Echoing Silence

Echoing Silence

THOMAS MERTON
on the Vocation of Writing

• • •

EDITED WITH AN INTRODUCTION BY

Robert Inchausti

NEW SEEDS
Boston & London
2007

New Seeds Books
An imprint of Shambhala Publications, Inc.
Horticultural Hall
300 Massachusetts Avenue
Boston, Massachusetts 02115
www.newseedsbooks.com

© 2007 Robert Inchausti

9 8 7 6 5 4 3 2 1

FIRST EDITION

Designed by Lora Zorian

Printed in the United States of America

⊗ This edition is printed on acid-free paper that meets
the American National Standards Institute Z39.48 Standard.
Distributed in the United States by Random House, Inc.,
and in Canada by Random House of Canada Ltd

LIBRARY OF CONGRESS CATALOGING-IN-PUBLICATION DATA
Echoing silence: Thomas Merton on the vocation of
writing/edited with an introduction by Robert Inchausti.
    p. cm.
Includes bibliographical references.
ISBN-13: 978-1-59030-348-1 (pbk.: alk. paper)
1. Merton, Thomas, 1915–1968. 2. Authorship—Religious aspects—
Christianity. 3. Vocation—Christianity. I. Inchausti, Robert, 1952–
BX4705.M542E24 2007
808'.02—dc22
2006029821

CONTENTS

Introduction   vii

Sources and Abbreviations   xi

Writing as a Spiritual Calling   1

The Christian Writer in the
    Modern World   31

On Poetry   81

On Other Writers   101

On His Own Writing   155

Advice to Writers   197

Acknowledgments   211

INTRODUCTION

The object of writing is to grow a personality
which in the end enables one to transcend art.

LAWRENCE DURRELL—*Balthazar*

THOMAS MERTON began writing as a teenager in an
effort to discover who he was and what he believed.
This discipline transformed him from a self-confessed
middle-class prig into a struggling bohemian artist seeking
to forge in the smithy of his soul the uncreated conscience
of his race.

But in the process of writing his Joycean novels and
poems, the young Merton transformed himself into the vir-
tual opposite of what he intended to become—moving
through the demanding integrity of art into the even more
demanding integrity of Christian asceticism.

"We do not have to create a conscience for ourselves,"
he later wrote. "We are born with one, and no matter how
much we may ignore it, we cannot silence its insistent demand that we do good and avoid evil." (NM 41–42) He
converted to Catholicism in 1938 and joined a Trappist
order in 1941.

When Merton entered the monastery, he thought he had turned his back on the literary life forever. He sent his unpublished manuscripts back to his former college professor Mark Van Doren, fully expecting to write little, if anything, ever again.

This turned out to be a short-lived resolution. He continued to write poetry in the monastery as a morning meditation, and he was given writing assignments by the abbot. One of his autobiographical essays, blossomed into the international best seller *The Seven Storey Mountain* (1948).

And yet despite his success as a writer, or perhaps because of it, Merton became more troubled than ever by the seeming incompatibility of his literary life with his vocation as a monk. "The artist," he wrote, "enters into himself in order to work. But the mystic enters into himself, not in order to work, but to pass through the center of his soul and lose himself in the mystery and secrecy and infinite, transcendent reality of God living and working within him." (LE 350)

But after reading the literature of mystics, particularly Saint John of the Cross, Merton came to see that the mystic and artist were not mutually exclusive callings. The work of the artist, like the work of the peasant, can lead to the fullness of Being. And so Merton continued to write religious devotions, journals, and poetry well into the 1950s—exploring the existential dimensions of Thomist theology and the experience of contemplation. The signature book from this period was his devotional classic *Seeds of Contemplation*.

Soon Merton was corresponding with a host of influential contemporary artists and thinkers—everyone from Erich Fromm and Boris Pasternak to Hans Urs von Balthasar and Daniel Berrigan. As the sixties unfolded, Thomas Merton was changing, unpacking his mind and shedding whatever false piety he might have aqiured as a cloistered monk. His book of social criticism *Conjectures of a Guilty Bystander* (1966) signaled his full transformation from a mere Catholic apologist to a contemplative culture critic whose essays built a bridge from the sacred to the secular and from the modern to the millennial mind.

Merton's writing from this period possessed an apocalyptic dimension that made him a decidedly different kind of social critic than any of his contemporaries. For him, time was not the unfolding of evolutionary developments or the empty movement of atoms into ever-more complex forms. It was, rather, a trail of blood and suffering that called for repentance, charity, and sacrifice. As a consequence, his works were more theologically mature than his literary peers Jack Kerouac and Henry Miller and more in touch with the realities of his times than those of his Catholic cohorts Jacques Maritain and Jean Leclerq.

The last four years of his life, Merton lived alone in a hermitage in the woods and continued his dialogues with different religious and intellectual traditions. This last phase was cut short by his accidental death in Bangkok in 1968. His writings and speeches from this time, excerpts of which are included here, suggest that he was changing themes yet again: moving from someone at odds with his age to someone openly living within its paradoxes and contradictions—exposing the soulless tautologies of our systematically distorted, communication systems.

This book tells the story of how Thomas Merton progressed from an inwardly divided modernist to a stylistic innovator who used language reflexively to construct a critique of itself. And though he moved in and out of particular interests, phases, roles, and themes, what is most consistent—what defines his attitude, orientation, style, and contribution—is his perennial return to origins, to emptiness, and to God.

Introduction

Merton's journey reminds us that if we transcend the horizon of our common humanity, we haven't really gone anywhere at all. One transgresses only to return, and one returns to the place from which one started for the very first time. This place is the abode of the great I AM—the "I" of the "I." And once we recover it, we cease fussing about the divine mystery and become one with it.

Merton never really left the literary life behind, but he did see through its pretensions from the far side of the monastery wall, and this, in the end, allowed him to grow a personality (his presence as a person) that in the end allowed him to transcend art and narrow sectarianism. In the process, he translated the "insider" speech of Catholic monasticism into the "universal" language of personal candor and existential revelation.

Thomas Merton brought contemplation into the twentieth century, divesting it of its antique scholasticism and ancient prejudices: making it efficient far beyond the inner circle of Christian initiates. He retained the best that was thought and said within the monastic counter culture—preserving its traditions while broadening its appeal and bringing it into dialogue with the contemporary world.

Merton's writings *on writing* show us how we might do the same. In a postsecular age increasingly beset by fast faith and false art and rapidly dividing into "tiny colonies of the saved," I can think of few more useful or important lessons.

Robert Inchausti
San Luis Obispo,
California, 2006

SOURCES AND ABBREVIATIONS

AJ   *The Asian Journal of Thomas Merton,* edited by
          Naomi Burton, Patrick Hart, and James Laugh-
          lin (New York: New Directions, 1973).

BOT   *The Behavior of Titans* (New York: New Direc-
          tions, 1961).

CABLES   *Cables to the Ace, or Familiar Liturgies of Misun-
          derstanding* (New York: New Directions, 1967).

CFT   *The Courage for Truth: The Letters of Thomas
          Merton to Writers,* selected and edited by Chris-
          tine M. Bochen (New York: Farrar, Straus &
          Giroux, 1993).

CGB   *Conjectures of a Guilty Bystander* (Garden City,
          N.Y.: Doubleday, 1966).

CP   *The Collected Poems of Thomas Merton* (New
          York: New Directions, 1977).

DQ   *Disputed Questions* (San Diego: Harcourt Brace
          Jovanovich, 1985).

ETS   *Entering the Silence: The Journals of Thomas Mer-
          ton, Volume Two 1941–1952,* edited by Jonathan
          Montaldo (San Francisco: HarperCollins, 1997).

HGL   *The Hidden Ground of Love: Letters on Religions
          Experience and Social Concerns,* edited by

William H. Shannon (New York: Harcourt Brace Jovanovich, 1985).

HR   *"Honorable Reader": Reflections on My Work,* edited by Robert E. Daggy (New York: Crossroad, 1991).

IE   *The Inner Experience: Notes on Contemplation,* edited and with an introduction by William H. Shannon (San Francisco: HarperCollins, 2003).

LE   *The Literary Essays of Thomas Merton,* edited by Patrick Hart (New York: New Directions, 1981).

MAWG   *My Argument with the Gestapo* (Garden City, N.Y.: Doubleday, 1969).

NM   *No Man Is an Island* (New York: Harcourt Brace Jovanovich, 1983).

NS   *New Seeds of Contemplation* (New York: New Directions, 1972).

NVA   *The Nonviolent Alternative,* edited by Gordon C. Zahn (New York: Farrar, Straus & Giroux, 1971).

RTJ   *The Road to Joy: The Letters of Thomas Merton to New and Old Friends,* selected and edited by Robert E. Daggy (New York: Farrar, Straus, & Giroux, 1989).

RU   *Raids on the Unspeakable* (New York: New Directions, 1966).

RUN   *Run to the Mountain: The Journals of Thomas Merton, Volume One 1939–1941,* edited by Patrick Hart (San Francisco: HarperCollins, 1995).

SOC   *The School of Charity: The Letters of Thomas Merton on Religious Renewal and Spiritual Direction,* selected and edited by Patrick Hart (New York: Farrar, Straus & Giroux, 1990).

SOJ   *The Sign of Jonas* (San Diego: Harcourt Brace Jovanovich, 1979).

SSM   *The Seven Storey Mountain* (San Diego: Harcourt Brace Jovanovich, 1976).

TMJL   *Thomas Merton and James Laughlin: Selected Letters,* edited by David D. Cooper (New York: Norton, 1997).

TMR   *A Thomas Merton Reader,* edited by Thomas P. McDonnell (New York: Doubleday, 1974).

WHEN   *When Prophecy Still Had a Voice: The Letters of Thomas Merton and Robert Lax,* edited by Arthur W. Biddle (Lexington: University Press of Kentucky, 2001).

WOC   *The Way of Chuang Tzu* (New York: New Directions, 1965).

WOD   *The Wisdom of the Desert* (New York: New Directions, 1960).

WTF   *Witness to Freedom: Letters in Times of Crisis,* selected and edited by William H. Shannon (New York: Farrar, Straus & Giroux, 1994).

Echoing Silence

Writing as a Spiritual Calling

From The Seven Storey Mountain, *1948*

I WANTED TO BE A WRITER, a poet, a critic, a professor. I wanted to enjoy all kinds of pleasures of the intellect and of the senses, and in order to have these pleasures I did not hesitate to place myself in situations which I knew would end in spiritual disaster—although generally I was so blinded by my own appetites that I never even clearly considered this fact until it was too late, and the damage was done.

Of course, as far as my ambitions went, their objects were all right in themselves. There is nothing wrong in being a writer or a poet—at least I hope there is not: but the harm lies in wanting to be one for the gratification of one's own ambitions, and merely in order to bring oneself up to the level demanded by his own internal self-idolatry. Because I was writing for myself and for the world, the things I wrote were rank with the passions and selfishness and sin from which they sprang. An evil tree brings forth evil fruits, when it brings forth fruit at all.

I went to Mass, of course, not merely every Sunday, but sometimes during the week as well. I was never long from the Sacraments—usually I went to confession and Communion if not every week, every fortnight. I did a fair amount of reading that might be called "spiritual" although I did not read spiritually. I devoured books, making notes here and there and remembering whatever I thought would be useful in an argument—that is, for my own aggrandizement, in order that I myself might take these things and shine by their light, as if their truth belonged to me. And I occasionally made a visit to a church in the afternoons, to pray or do the Stations of the Cross.

All this would have been enough for an ordinary Catholic, with a lifetime of faithful practice of his religion behind him: but for me it could not possibly be enough. A man who has just come out of the hospital, having nearly died there and having been cut to pieces on an operating table, cannot immediately begin to lead the life of an ordinary working man. And after the spiritual mangle I have gone through, it will never be possible for me to do without the Sacraments daily, and without much prayer and penance and meditation and mortification.

It took me time to find it out: but I write down what I have found out at last, so that anyone who is now in the position that I was in then may read it and know what to do to save himself from great peril and unhappiness. And to such a one I would say:

Whoever you are, the land to which God has brought you is not like the land of Egypt from which you came out. You can no longer live here as you lived there. Your old life and your former ways are crucified now, and you must not seek to live anymore for your own gratification, but give up your own judgment into the hands of a wise director, and sacrifice your pleasures and comforts for the love of God and give the money you no longer spend on those things, to the poor.

Above all, eat your daily Bread without which you cannot live, and come to know Christ Whose Life feeds you in the Host, and He will give you a taste of joys and delights that transcend anything you have ever experienced before, and which will make the transition easy.

(SSM 231–32)

• • •

[Robert] Lax rebuked me for all this. Characteristically [Robert Lax] conceived the function of those who knew how to write, and who had something to say, in terms of the salvation of society. Lax's picture of America—before which he has stood for twelve years with his hands hanging in helplessness at his sides—is the picture of a country full of people who want to be kind and pleasant and happy and love good things and serve God, but do not know how. And they do not know where to turn to find out. They are surrounded by all kinds of sources of information which only conspire to bewilder them more and more. And Lax's vision is a vision of the day when they will turn on the radio and somebody will start telling them what they have really been wanting to hear and needing to know. They will find somebody who is capable of telling them of the love of God in language that will no longer sound hackneyed or crazy, but with authority and conviction: the conviction born of sanctity.

I am not sure whether this conception of his necessarily implies a specific vocation, a definite and particular mission: but in any case, he assumed that it was the sort of thing that should be open to me, to [Bob] Gibney, to Seymour [Freedgood], to Mark Van Doren, to some writers he admired, perhaps even to somebody who did not know how to talk, but could only play a trumpet or a piano. And it was open to himself also: but for himself, he was definitely waiting to be "sent."

In any case, although I had gone before him to the fountains of grace, Lax was much wiser than I, and had clearer vision, and was, in fact, corresponding much more truly to the grace of God than I, and he had seen what was the only important thing. I think he has told what he had to say to many people besides myself: but certainly his was one of the voices through which the insistent Spirit of God was determined to teach me the way I had to travel.

Therefore, another one of those times that turned out to be historical, as far as my own soul is concerned, was when Lax and I were walking down Sixth Avenue, one night in the spring. The street was all torn up and trenched and banked high with dirt and marked out with red lanterns where they were digging the subway, and we picked our way along the fronts of the dark little stores, going downtown to Greenwich Village. I forget what we were arguing about, but in the end Lax suddenly turned around and asked me the question:

"What do you want to be, anyway?"

I could not say, "I want to be Thomas Merton the well-known writer of all those book reviews in the back pages of the *Times Book Review*," or "Thomas Merton the assistant instructor of Freshman English at the New Life Social Institute for Progress and Culture," so I put the thing on the spiritual plane, where I knew it belonged and said:

"I don't know; I guess what I want is to be a good Catholic."

"What do you mean, you want to be a good Catholic?"

The explanation I gave was lame enough, and expressed my confusion, and betrayed how little I had really thought about it at all.

Lax did not accept it.

"What you should say"—he told me—"what you should say is that you want to be a saint."

A saint! The thought struck me as a little weird. *I* said: "How do you expect me to become a saint?"

"By wanting to," said Lax, simply.

"I can't be a saint," I said, "I can't be a saint." And my mind darkened with a confusion of realities and unrealities: the knowledge of my own sins, and the false humility which makes men say that they cannot do the things that they *must* do, cannot reach the level that they *must* reach: the cowardice that says: "I am satisfied to save my soul, to keep out of mortal sin," but which means, by those words: "I do not want to give up my sins and my attachments."

(SSM 236–37)

• • •

I knelt at the altar rail in the little Mexican church of Our Lady of Guadalupe on Fourteenth Street, where I sometimes went to Communion, and asked with great intensity of desire for the publication of the book,[1] if it should be for God's glory.

The fact that I could even calmly assume that there was some possibility of the book giving glory to God shows the profound depths of my ignorance and spiritual blindness: but anyway, that was what I asked. But now I realize that it was a very good thing that I made that prayer.

1. The "book" Merton is referring to here is his unpublished first novel initially titled *The Straits of Dover,* then *The Night before the Battle,* and finally *The Labyrinth.*—Ed.

It is a matter of common belief among Catholics that when God promises to answer our prayers, He does not promise to give us exactly what we ask for. But we can always be certain that if He does not give us that, it is because He has something much better to give us instead. That is what is meant by Christ's promise that we will receive all that we ask in His Name. *Quodcumque petimus adversus utilitatem salutis, non petimus in nomine Salvatoris.*

I think I prayed as well as I could, considering what I was, and with considerable confidence in God and in Our Lady, and I knew I would be answered. I am only just beginning to realize how well I was answered. In the first place the book was never published, and that was a good thing. But in the second place God answered me by a favor which I had already refused and had practically ceased to desire. He gave me back the vocation that I had half-consciously given up, and He opened to me again the doors that had fallen shut when I had not known what to make of my Baptism and the grace of that First Communion.

But before He did this I had to go through some little darkness and suffering.

I think those days at the end of August 1939 were terrible for everyone. They were grey days of great heat and sultriness and the weight of physical oppression by the weather added immeasurably to the burden of the news from Europe that got more ominous day by day.

(SSM 247)

Journal Entry, January 15, 1941

I RENOUNCE with the greatest alacrity in the world the following literary projects:

1. Writing a story about a man who owns a dog named *Caesar*—the whole purpose of this story would be to have

someone come in with a pail of old bones and garbage and pieces of gristle, and chicken guts, and melon-rinds etc. etc. and say, "What am I supposed to do with all these old bones, etc.?"

To which the man would wittily reply: "Give unto Caesar the things that are Caesar's," or rather "Render—etc."

2. Writing a story about a bantamweight prizefighter named "Kid Promiscuous."

3. Drawing a cartoon having the following caption: "Where was you, playing volleyball?"

4. Writing a literary article beginning—"I fear me there is a little of the Helen Hokinson in every one of us, and each literary genius, if he only allowed himself, could reveal himself to the world with as dull an imagination as that of Gluyas Williams." [*New Yorker* cartoonist]

5. Writing a radio speech that makes some sense. But I do not utterly renounce it, either.

6. Writing a story about four people, two old and two young, models who had never seen each other before, and who had to pose for a big color-photo for an advertising agency, as if they were a family, father, mother, daughter, grandson—or some child.

7. Another literary article beginning: "Every man a Coleridge! Fill your journals with worthless projects! See what jolly sport!"

8. I never renounced, because I never thought of, the idea of writing a story about some people in an air raid shelter during an air raid. Now I have thought of the idea, and now I renounce it.

The story about a revolution on some Caribbean Island,

which was to have been a *Collier's* story, was renounced in June 1939 and stays renounced. The Island was called San Jamie. I renounce the *Collier's* story as a literary form for me, forever.

(RUN 289–90)

From Journal of My Escape from the Nazis

In this except from Merton's early novel Journal of My Escape from the Nazis *(now titled* My Argument with the Gestapo*), Merton's protagonist is confronted by British soldiers during the London blitz.*

SUDDENLY, ACROSS THE STREET, on the opposite pavement, stand two men pointing at my window. They are men in dark suits and helmets. The suits are blue serge, and well pressed, too. They have seen me, sitting not far from the window, typewriting. They do not like me, sitting in one of the bombed houses of London, writing on my typewriter.

Now they see me looking at them and writing on my typewriter. They both fold their arms and frown at me from under their helmets.

I stare back at them.

They speak to one another, over there. I see their heads nodding.

Then one of them raises his head, and his voice comes to me easily across the quiet street, without any necessity for shouting:

"You in the window," it says, "is your house empty, or occupied? And if it is empty, what are you doing, type-writing in an empty house?"

"It is occupied," I say. "Can't you see I am in it?"

"It is our business to know which houses are occupied. This is the house of Madame Gongora: has she left it, or is she still living there?"

"She is still here."

"Are you her secretary?"

"I am a writer. I write what I see out of the window. I am writing about the fear on the faces of the houses. I say as fast as I can, what preoccupation I see in the sick houses of bombarded London, and I write that the houses of bombarded London do not understand their own fear."

My words fall into the street with absolutely no echo at all, as clear as if I were talking to myself, and, just as clear and distinct to my ear come the quietly spoken words of the man in the helmet.

"What have you just written about us? Have you written about our courage?"

"I have written that you folded your arms and frowned at me from under the shadows of your helmets. I have not written about your courage."

Now they whisper to one another, again, their heads nod until they turn again to where I am. The other one says (the one who had not spoken before):

"Who are you working for? Why do you write that our houses do not understand their fear: rather write that they do not understand their courage."

"It is the same thing."

"Then what do you know about our courage and our fear? Where do you come from? What is the basis of your statements about us? You say you write what you see, but no two men see the same street, here. What do you see that you write? What do you mean when you talk about our courage and our fear?"

"I am still trying to find out: and that is why I write."

"How will you find out by writing?"

"I will keep putting things down until they become clear."

"And if they do not become clear?"

"I will have a hundred books, full of symbols, full of everything I ever knew or ever saw or ever thought."

"If it never becomes clear, perhaps you will have more books than if it were all clear at once."

"No doubt. But I say if it were all clear at once, I would not really understand it, either. Some things are too clear to be understood, and what you think is your understanding of them is only a kind of charm, a kind of incantation in your mind concerning that thing. This is not understanding: it is something you remember. So much for definitions! We always have to go back and start from the beginning and make over all the definitions for ourselves again."

(MAWG 52–53)

Journal Entry, September 3, 1941

THERE IS NOTHING WRONG with praying to be, as a writer, as everything, obscure, unknown.

There is everything wrong with praying to be a bad writer.

I would pray to be the best writer of a certain time and never to know it, and to be also the most obscure. Saint Therese probably never even considered herself a writer. Bloy was one of the best writers in a time when there were some good writers: and also the most despised, one of the most obscure: "*L'Invendable*."

But I am not here [in the monastery] to think about being a writer: except I am here to try to learn humility and how to do God's will and serve Him the best way I can, and writing has something to do with all these things, accidentally, because it happens that I like to write, and try to know how.

(RUN 397)

From a Letter to Robert Lax, November 21, 1942

NATURALLY, WHILE SOMETIMES you are very quiet and happy because God is very obviously with you, with a presence & blessedness you never imagined possible, at other times this is not so. Then you try to pray or think of Christ and your mind instead of filling with peace, fills with slogans, He-she jokes, movies so bad you had forgotten them by the self-protective work of your own subconscious mind. You think of million dollar advertising ideas, and this makes you very ashamed, and bored, & disgusted. This is a trial common to our life, & has good effects, one of the principal of which is to make you love God not only for His obvious gifts, but realizing clearly, by His apparent absence, how infinitely preferable He is to everything else. That this absence is only apparent is clear from St. John of the Cross, and all the others, & everybody here knows it perfectly well, and really, you feel bad some days, but it is nothing to the bad days you had outside, in the world. Also, as soon as this is done with, your mind unexpectedly fills up with the presence of God twice as real and twice as holy as before. For another result of these temptations is to make you very docile, very detached from your own opinions and judgments & way of doing things, and then you rely on God for the smallest things, for every thing. And this is peace, because God gives everybody everything, & the only reason each person doesn't have more is that he gets in God's way, trying to get things with our own dumb will.

(WHEN 90)

From a Letter to Mark Van Doren, March 30, 1948

I CAN NO LONGER SEE the ultimate meaning of a man's life in terms of either "being a poet" or "being a contemplative" or even in a certain sense in "being a saint" (although that is the only thing to be). It must be something much more immediate than that. I—and every other person in the world—must say: "I have my own special, peculiar destiny which no one else ever has had or ever will have. There exists for me a particular goal, a fulfillment which must be all my own—nobody else's—& it does not really identify that destiny to put it under some category—'poet,' 'monk,' 'hermit.' Because my own individual destiny is a meeting, an encounter with God that He has destined for me alone. His glory in me will be to receive from me something He can never receive from anyone else—because it is a gift of His to me which He has never given to anyone else & never will. My whole life is only that—to establish that particular constant with God which is the one He has planned for my eternity!"

Once that contact is established—I feel it in my bones & it sets me on fire—the possibilities are *without end.* Unlimited fruitfulness, life, productivity, vision, peace. Yet I have no way of saying just what it will be. I don't think it will be merely writing & I don't think it will be anything I have ever yet known as contemplation & in fact I don't think it will be anything that anyone on earth can see or understand—especially myself.

In the light of all that, it doesn't make so much sense anymore to be planning to either renounce or to adopt whole "blocks" of activity—cutting out "all" writing or "going into solitude for good" (as I would like to)—the thing is to take a new line & let everything be determined by immediate circumstances that manifest God's will & His action here & now. No matter where it may seem to lead, because I don't really know anyway & I don't have to know provided that God is doing the leading.

(RTJ 22–23)

Journal Entry, October 10, Sunday, 1948

S OONER OR LATER the world must burn, and all things in it—all the books, the cloister together with the brothel, Fra Angelico together with the Lucky Strike ads which I haven't seen for seven years because I don't remember seeing one in Louisville. Sooner or later it will all be consumed by fire and nobody will be left—for by that time the last man in the universe will have discovered the bomb capable of destroying the universe and will have been unable to resist the temptation to throw the thing and get it over with.

And here I sit writing a diary.

But love laughs at the end of the world because love is the door to eternity and he who loves God is playing on the doorstep of eternity, and before anything can happen love will have drawn him over the sill and closed the door and he won't bother about the world burning because he will know nothing but love.

(SOJ 122)

Journal Entry, July 20, 1949

I AM FINDING MYSELF forced to admit that my lamentations about my writing job have been foolish. At the moment the writing is the one thing that gives me access to some real silence and solitude. Also I find that it helps me to pray because, when I pause at my work, I find that the mirror inside me is surprisingly clean and deep and serene and God shines there and is immediately found, without hunting, as if He had come close to me while I was writing and I had not observed His coming. And this I think should be the cause of great joy, and to me it is.

(ETS 338)

Journal Entry, September 1, 1949

I NOW KNOW THAT all my own poems about the world's suffering have been inadequate: they have not solved anything, they have only camouflaged the problem. And it seems to me that the urge to write a real poem about suffering and sin is only another temptation because, after all, I do not really understand.

Sometimes I feel that I would like to stop writing, precisely as a gesture of defiance. In any case, I hope to stop publishing for a time, for I believe it has now become impossible for me to stop writing altogether. Perhaps I shall continue writing on my deathbed, and even take some asbestos paper with me in order to go on writing in purgatory. Except that I hope Our Lady will arrange some miraculous victory over my sins that will make purgatory unnecessary.

And yet it seems to me that writing, far from being an obstacle to spiritual perfection in my own life, has become one of the conditions on which my perfection will depend. If I am to be a saint—and there is nothing else that I can think of desiring to be—it seems that I must get there by writing books in a Trappist monastery. If I am to be a saint, I have not only to be a monk, which is what all monks must do to become saints, but I must also put down on paper what I have become. It may sound simple, but it is not an easy vocation.

To be as good a monk as I can, and to remain myself,

and to write about it: to put myself down on paper, in such a situation, with the most complete simplicity and integrity—masking nothing, confusing no issue: this is very hard, because I am all mixed up in illusions and attachments. These, too, will have to be put down. But without exaggeration, repetition, useless emphasis.' No need for breast-beating and lamentation before the eyes of anyone but You, O God, who see the depths of my fatuity. To be frank without being boring. It is a kind of crucifixion. Not a very dramatic or painful one. But it requires so much honesty that it is beyond my nature. It must come somehow from the Holy Ghost.

One of the results of all this could well be a complete and holy transparency: living, praying, and writing in the light of the Holy Spirit, losing myself entirely by becoming public property just as Jesus is public property in the Mass. Perhaps this is an important aspect of my priesthood—my living of my Mass: to become as plain as a Host in the hands of everybody. Perhaps it is this, after all, that is to be my way of solitude. One of the strangest ways so far devised, but it is the way of the Word of God.

Yet, after all, this only teaches me that nothing vital about myself can ever be public property!

(SOJ 233–34)

Journal Entry, December 14, 1949

THE BEST THING for me is a lucid silence that does not even imagine it speaks to anybody. A silence in which I see no interlocutor, frame no message for anyone, formulate no word either for man or paper. There will still be plenty to say when the time comes to write, and what is written will be simpler and more fruitful.

(SOJ 258)

Journal Entry, December 22, 1949

THERE IS A CONVERSION of the deep will to God that cannot be effected in words—barely in a gesture or ceremony. There is a conversion of the deep will and a gift of my substance that is too mysterious for liturgy, and too private. It is something to be done in a lucid secrecy that implies first of all the denial of communication to others except perhaps as a neutral thing.

I shall remember the time and place of this liberty and this neutrality which cannot be written down. These clouds low on the horizon, the outcrops of hard yellow rock in the road, the open gate, the perspective of fence-posts leading up the rise to the sky, and the big cedars tumbled and tousled by the wind. Standing on rock. Present. The reality of the present and of solitude divorced from past and future. To be collected and gathered up in clarity and silence and to belong to God and to be nobody else's business. I wish I could recover the liberty of that interior decision which was very simple and which seems to me to have been a kind of blank check and a promise.

(SOJ 252–53)

• • •

I seek no face, I treasure no experience, no memory. Anything I write down here is only for personal guidance because of my constant gravitation away from solitude. It will remind me how to go home. Not to be like the man who looked in the glass and straightaway forgot what manner of man he was; yet I shall not remember myself in such a way that I remember the person I am not.

(SOJ 253–54)

• • •

They can have Thomas Merton. He's dead. Father Louis—he's half dead too. For my part *my* name is that sky, those fence-posts, and those cedar trees. I shall not even reflect on who I am and I shall not say my identity is nobody's business because that implies a truculence I don't intend. It has no meaning.

(SOJ 253)

Journal Entry, April 14, 1950

How can a man really know whether to write or not, whether to speak or not, whether his words and his silence are for good or for evil, for life or for death, unless he understands the two divisions of tongues—the division of Babel, when men were scattered in their speech because of pride, and the division of Pentecost when the Holy Ghost sent out men of one dialect to speak all the languages of the earth and bring all men to unity: that they may be one, Father, Thou in Me and one in Them that they may be one in us!

(SOJ 299)

From a Letter to Dom Jean-Baptiste Porion, February 9, 1952

Dom Jean-Baptiste Porion was a Carthusian monk of La Grande Chartreuse in southern France and author of The Prayer of Love and Silence.

For my own part, as you know, the betrayal of our deep self that sometimes takes place in our effort to communicate with others exteriorly, has long been a problem. It is not easy for a writer to learn to live, interiorly, without a witness, without a potential reader. But once this intruder is expelled, we truly find ourselves, and find God—and find other men in God. We betray ourselves and one another in the No Man's Land which exists between human beings, and into which they go out to meet one another disguised in words. And yet without words we cannot find ourselves, without communication with men we do not know God: *fides ex auditu* [faith comes from hearing]. You have justly assessed the balance that must be preserved between the two—so that the word of faith that is passed from one soul to the secrecy of another soul matures in both and grows into understanding: and flowers in God alone. . . .

The only writing I do now is in the form of maxims—sometimes they seem to be a little like Guigo.[2] I think he is very fine. I like his lapidary quality. I find myself beginning to use these maxims for direction [with the scholastics]. I write one out—for instance a word or two of Latin—and slip it to them a day or two before they come to see me. They can think about the words, enter into them, and give me something of their own in return, so that I hope in time that direction of my best scholastics will become nothing more than a few cries—as of angels hailing one another briefly from cliff to cliff on the walls of the mountain leading to heaven. Here are several of the Latin maxims—for you on *your* cliff:

2. Guigo II, a Carthusian monk, wrote the *Scala Paradiso* (or *Scala Claustralium*), about the contemplative life, in 1150 A.D., just before Saint Bernard's death. It was translated into Middle English for the Latin-less contemplative, Brother Gervase.—Ed.

Solitudo pauperis quievit in potestate Altissimi!
[The solitude of the poor man rests on the power
      of God!]

*Silentium coelorum sit mihi lex: et vita mea imago lu-
minis.*
[Let the silence of heaven be my law: and my life an
      image of light.]

Nomen meum eructavit caritas ex profundis.
[Charity uttered my name from the depths.]

Fons vitae silentium in corde noctis.
[A fountain of life is silence in the heart of night.]

It would make a nice monastic book—the first monastic one I shall have done—to produce these, with brief
meditations on them in English. Perhaps twenty or thirty
maxims, with meditations: not more than a hundred pages
in all.

(SOC 32–34)

From No Man Is an Island *(1955)*

SILENCE DOES NOT EXIST in our lives merely for its own
sake. It is ordered to something else. Silence is the
mother of speech. A lifetime of silence is ordered to an ultimate declaration, which can be put into words, a declaration of all we have lived for.

Life and death, words and silence, are given us because
of Christ. In Christ we die to the flesh and live to the spirit.
In Him we die to illusion and live to truth. We speak to
confess Him, and we are silent in order to meditate on Him
and enter deeper into His silence, which is at once the si-

lence of death and of eternal life—the silence of Good Friday night and the peace of Easter morning.

(NM 258–59)

From "Poetry and Contemplation: A Reappraisal," October 24, 1958

IT IS THE COMMON DOCTRINE of Christian mystical theologians that a great obstacle to "unitive" or "connatural" or "affective" knowledge of God by infused contemplation (the terms are those of St. Thomas and his followers) is attachment to objectivized human reasoning and analysis and discourse that proceeds by abstraction from sense images, and by syllogizing, to conclusions. In other words, a man cannot at the same time fly in an airplane and walk along the ground. He must do one or the other. And if he insists on walking along the ground—all right, it is no sin. But it will take him much longer and cost him much more effort to get to his destination, and he will have a much more limited view of things along his way.

What the Holy Spirit demands of the mystic is peaceful consent and a blind trust in Him: for all this time, since the soul does not act of itself, it remains blind and in darkness, having no idea where it is going or what is being done, and tasting satisfaction that is, at first, extremely tenuous and ineffable and obscure. The reason is, of course, that the soul is not yet sufficiently spiritualized to be able to grasp and appreciate what is going on within it. It remains with nothing but the vaguest and most general sense that God is really and truly present and working there—a sense which is fraught with a greater certitude than anything it has ever experienced before. And yet if one stops to analyze the experience, or if one makes a move to increase its intensity by a natural act, the whole thing will evade his grasp and he will lose it altogether.

Now it is precisely here that the aesthetic instinct changes its colors and, from being a precious gift, becomes a real danger. If the intuition of the poet naturally leads him into the inner sanctuary of his soul, it is for a special purpose in the natural order: when the poet enters into himself, it is in order to reflect upon his inspiration and to clothe it with a special and splendid form and then return to *display it to those outside*. And here the radical difference between the artist and the mystic begins to be seen. The artist enters into himself in order to *work*. For him, the "superior" soul is a forge where inspiration kindles a fire of white heat, a crucible for the transformation of natural images into new, created forms. But the mystic enters into himself, not in order to work but to pass through the center of his own soul and lose himself in the mystery and secrecy and infinite, transcendent reality of God living and working within him.

Consequently, if the mystic happens to be, at the same time, an artist, when prayer calls him within himself to the secrecy of God's presence, his art will be tempted to start working and producing and studying the "creative" possibilities of this experience. And therefore immediately the whole thing runs the risk of being frustrated and destroyed. The artist will run the risk of losing a gift of tremendous supernatural worth, in order to perform a work of far less value. He will let go of the deep, spiritual grace which has been granted him, in order to return to the reflection of that grace within his own soul. He will withdraw from the mystery of identification with Reality beyond forms and objectivized concepts, and will return to the realm of subject and object. He will objectivize his own experience and seek to exploit and employ it for its own sake. He will leave God and return to himself, and in so doing, though he follows his natural instinct to "create," he will, in fact, be less creative. For the creative work done directly in the soul and on the soul by God Himself, the infinite *Creator Spiritus,* is beyond all comparison with the work which the soul of man itself accomplishes in imitation of the divine Creator.

Unable fully to lose himself in God, doomed by the restlessness of talent to seek himself in the highest natural gift that God has given him, the artist falls from contemplation and returns to himself as artist. Instead of passing through his own soul into the abyss of the infinite actuality of God Himself, he will remain there a moment, only to emerge again into the exterior world of multiple created things whose variety once more dissipates his energies until they are lost in perplexity and dissatisfaction.

There is, therefore, a likelihood that one who has the natural gift of artistic intuition and creation may be unable to pass on to the superior and most spiritual kind of contemplation, in which the soul rests in God without images, without concepts, without any intermediary. The artist may be like the hare in the fable, who far outstrips the tortoise without talent in the beginnings of the contemplative life, but who, in the end, is left behind. In a word, natural gifts and talents may be of great value in the beginning, but contemplation can never depend on them. They may, indeed, prove to be obstacles, unless by some special grace we are completely detached from them. And so the artist may well receive the first taste of infused prayer, for, as St. John of the Cross says, that is granted to relatively many souls, and often quite soon in their spiritual life, especially where conditions are favorable: but, because of this tragic Promethean tendency to exploit every experience as material for "creation," the artist may remain there all his life on the threshold, never entering into the banquet, but always running back into the street to tell the passers-by of the wonderful music he has heard coming from inside the palace of the King!

(LE 350–51)

From The Inner Experience, *1959*

ONE OF THE STRANGE LAWS of the contemplative life is that in it you do not sit down and solve problems: you bear with them until they somehow solve themselves. Or until life itself solves them for you. Usually the solution consists in a discovery that they only existed insofar as they were inseparably connected with your own illusory exterior self. The solution of most such problems comes with the dissolution of this false self. And consequently another law of the contemplative life is that if you enter it with the set purpose of seeking contemplation, or worse still, happiness, you will find neither. For neither can be found unless it is first in some sense renounced. And again, this means renouncing the illusory self that seeks to be "happy" and to find "fulfillment" (whatever that may mean) in contemplation. For the contemplative and spiritual self, the dormant, mysterious, and hidden self that is always effaced by the activity of our exterior self does not seek fulfillment. It is content to *be,* and in its being it is fulfilled, because its being is rooted in God.

(IE 2–3)

From a Letter to Victor Hammer, *May 14, 1959*

Victor Hammer was an artist born in Vienna in 1882; he moved to the United States during the Second World War.

T HE BEAUTY OF ALL CREATION is a reflection of Sophia living and hidden in creation. But it is only our reflection. And the misleading thing about beauty, created beauty, is that we expect Sophia to be simply a more intense and more perfect and more brilliant, un-spoiled, spiritual revelation of the same beauty. Whereas to arrive at her beauty we must pass through an apparent negation of created beauty, and to reach her light we must realize that in comparison with created light it is a dark-ness. But this is only because created beauty and light are ugliness and darkness compared with her. Again the whole thing is in the question of mercy, which cuts across the divisions and passes beyond every philosophical and religious ideal. For Sophia is not an ideal, not an abstrac-tion, but the highest reality, and the highest reality must manifest herself to us not only in power but also in poverty, otherwise we never see it. Sophia is the Lady Poverty to whom St. Francis was married. And of course she dwelt with the Desert Fathers in their solitude, for it was she who brought them there and she whom they knew there. It was with her that they conversed all the time in their silence.

(WTF 5)

From "Notes for Philosophy of Solitude," 1960

WHY WRITE ABOUT SOLITUDE in the first place? Certainly not in order to preach it, to exhort people to become solitary. What could be more absurd? Those who are to become solitary are, as a rule, solitary already. At most they are not yet aware of their condition. In which case, all they need is to discover it. But in reality, all men are solitary. Only most of them are so averse to being alone, or to feeling alone, that they do everything they can to forget their solitude. How? Perhaps in large measure by what Pascal called "divertissement"—diversion, systematic distraction. By those occupations and recreations, so mercifully provided by society, which enable a man to avoid his own company for twenty-four hours a day.

(DQ 139)

From "Theology of Creativity," September–December 1960

THE CREATIVITY OF THE CHRISTIAN person must be seen in relation to the creative vocation of the new Adam, mystical person of the "whole Christ." The creative will of God has been at work in the cosmos since he said: "Let there be light." This creative *fiat* was not uttered merely at the dawn of time. All time and all history are a continued, uninterrupted creative act, a stupendous, ineffable mystery in which God has signified his will to associate man with himself in his work of creation. The will and power of the Almighty Father were not satisfied simply to make the world and turn it over to man to run it as best he could. The creative love of God was met, at first, by the destructive and self-centered refusal of man: an act of such incalculable consequences that it would have amounted to a destruction of God's plan, if that were possible. But the creative work of God could not be frustrated by man's sin. On the contrary, sin itself entered into that plan. If man was first called to share in the creative work of his heavenly Father, he now became involved in the "new creation," the redemption of his own kind and the restoration of the cosmos, purified and transfigured, into the hands of the Father. God himself became man in order that in this way man could be most perfectly associated with him in this great work, the fullest manifestation of his eternal wisdom and mercy.

(LE 369)

From the Introduction to
A Thomas Merton Reader, *1962*

I HAVE TRIED TO LEARN in my writing a monastic lesson I could probably not have learned otherwise: to let go of my idea of myself, to take myself with more than one grain of salt. If the monastic life is a life of hardship and sacrifice, I would say that for me most of the hardship has come in connection with writing. It is possible to doubt whether I have become a monk (a doubt I have to live with), but it is not possible to doubt that I am a writer, that I was born one and will most probably die as one. Disconcerting, dis-edifying as it is, this seems to be my lot and my vocation. It is what God has given me in order that I might give it back to Him.

(TMR 16)

From Conjectures
of a Guilty Bystander, *1966*

THE TRUE PHILOSOPHER and the true poet become what they are when they "go beyond" philosophy and poetry, and cease to "be philosophers" or to "be poets." It is at that point that their whole lives become philosophy and poetry—in other words, there is no longer any philosophy or any poetry separable from the unity of their existence. Philosophy and poetry have disappeared. The ordinary acts of everyday life—eating, sleeping, walking, etc., become philosophical acts which grasp the ultimate principles of life in life itself and not in abstraction.

From such unified existence come the aphorisms of great Asian contemplatives or Christian saints—and the poems of Zen masters.

(CGB 292)

• • •

This idea of a "writing career" which begins somewhere and ends somewhere is also a beautifully stupid fiction. Yet I can comfort myself with the idea that St. Thomas occupied his mind with it for a while, when he was my age. He told his secretary and biographer Reginald that if his days as a writer and teacher were over, then he wanted to die fast. I don't feel that way about it. And I don't feel that my days as a writer are over. I don't care where they are. The point for me is that I must stop trying to adjust myself to the fact that night will come and the work will end. So night comes. Then what? You sit in the dark. What is wrong with that? Meanwhile, it is time to give to others whatever I have to give and not reflect on it. I wish I had learned the knack of doing this without question or care. Perhaps I can begin. It is not a matter of adjustment or of peace. It is a matter of truth, and patience, and humility. Stop trying to "adjust."

Adjust to what? To the general fiction?

(CGB 264)

From a Letter to Robert Menchin, January 15, 1966

Menchin wrote to Merton about a project he was involved in, helping people make "career changes."

I HAD ALWAYS WANTED TO BE A WRITER. But one had to make a living and so I took up teaching (literature, college level) as a profession that would be favorable for writing. However, the idea of something more fundamental began to grow on me. The idea of a monastic vocation is something distinct from that of a "career." In a sense, you don't pick the monastic life, it picks you. In religious terms, that is expressed by saying that one believes oneself "called" by God to live a monastic life. Translated into ordinary language, this refers to a deep implosion which may even go against the grain of one's conscious inclinations. It entails a fight. There is a considerable amount of doubt and resistance, a great deal of questioning, and at times the whole thing seems absurd. Yet you have to push on with it. There is a sense of one's destiny and identity involved in this struggle.

For me, the monastic vocation even implied that I might have to give up writing, and when I finally decided to enter the Trappist Monastery of Gethsemani [Kentucky] I was reconciled with the idea of not writing anymore unless I was told to do so. As it happened, I was told to continue writing. But for me writing has always remained secondary. What has been important above all has been living in the most meaningful possible way, at least for me. This has meant, again, a lot of conflict, questioning, searching. Entering a monastery is only the beginning of a long road, not the end. People may imagine that the door of the monastery closes behind you and you go into nirvana. Not so. There is a lot of hard work to be done, many decisions to be made, and still many questions to answer. Many in the monastic life reach the point where they feel that they cannot go on, that they have reached a dead end. They then have to leave the monastery and start again (that is a difficult adjustment).

For my part, I have never for a moment questioned the vocation to be a monk, but I have had to settle many other questions about ways and means, the where and the how of being a monk. Consequently there has been a great deal of change in me, during the course of my monastic life. I would say that my interests have deepened and broadened as time went on. I have become more and more interested in all different forms of religious and monastic experiences, and it has been my privilege to engage in dialogue with men living according to Hinduism, Zen, Hasidic Judaism, Sufism, and so on. I have also become more deeply concerned with basic issues in the world situation. For me the monastery has not been a mere refuge: It has meant facing responsibility on the deepest level, and it has meant giving an account of myself to others, and being open to them in their problems.

Advice? I would say that there is one basic idea that should be kept in mind in all the changes we make in life, whether of career or anything else. We should decide not in view of better pay, higher rank, "getting ahead," but in view of becoming *more real,* entering more authentically into direct contact with life, living more as a free and mature human person, able to give myself more to others, able to understand myself and the world better. I hope these few notes may be of some use.

(WTF 254–55)

The Christian Writer in
the Modern World

From "The Tower of Babel," 1940

History is a dialogue between forward and
   backward
going inevitably forward by the misuse of
   words.
Now the function of the word is:
To designate first the machine,
Then what the machine produces
Then what the machine destroys.
Words show us these things not only in
   order to mean them
But in order to provoke them
And to incorporate us in their forward
   movement:
Doing, making, destroy or rather
Being done, being made, being destroyed.
Such is history.

The forgotten principle is that the machine
Should always destroy the maker of the
    machine
Being more important than the maker
Insofar as man is more important than God.
Words also reflect this principle
Though they are meant to conceal it
From the ones who are too young to know.

Thus words have no essential meaning.
They are means of locomotion
From backward to forward
Along an infinite horizontal plane,
Created by the history which they
    themselves destroy.
They are the makers of our only reality
The backward-forward working of the web
The movement into the web.

(CP 21–22)

From a Letter to Jean Leclercq, April 22, 1950

Dom Jean Leclercq (1911–1993) was a Benedictine monk and scholar of Clervaux, Luxembourg, and is the author of The Love of Learning and the Desire for God.

OUR STUDIES AND WRITING should by their very nature contribute to our contemplation at least remotely, and contemplation in turn should be able to find expression in channels laid open for it and deepened by familiarity with the Fathers of the Church. This is an age that calls for St. Augustines and Leos, Gregorys and Cyrils.

(SOC 1)

From "The Pasternak Affair," 1959

H ISTORY IS NOT A MATTER of inexorable scientific laws, it is a new creation, a work of God in and through man: but this theandric work is unthinkable not only without man's desire but also without his *initiative*. Christ has planted in the world the seeds of something altogether new, but they do not grow by themselves. Hence history has never yet really had a chance to become a Christian creation. For the world to be changed, man himself must begin to change it, he must take the initiative, he must step forth and make a new kind of history. The change begins within himself.

(LE 79)

From "Herakleitos: A Study," 1960

T HE WISE MAN must make tremendous efforts to grasp "the unexpected": that is to say he must keep himself alert, he must constantly "seek for himself," and he must not fear to strive for the excellence that will make him an object of hatred and mistrust in the eyes of the conventional majority—as did Hermodorus, whom the Ephesians threw out of their city on the ground that if he wanted to excel he had better go and do it somewhere else, for "we will have none who is best among us."

The aristocratic contempt of Herakleitos for the conventional verbalizing of his fellow citizens was something other than a pose, or a mad reflex of wounded sensibility. It was a prophetic manifestation of intransigent honesty. He refused to hold his peace and spoke out with angry concern for truth. He who had seen "the One" was no longer permitted to doubt, to hedge, to compromise, and to flatter. To treat his intuition as one among many opinions would have been inexcusable. False humility was an infidelity to his deepest self and a betrayal of the fundamental insights of his life. It would have been above all a betrayal of those whom he could not effectively contact except by the shock of paradox. Herakleitos took the same stand as Isaias, who was commanded by God to "blind the eyes of the people" by speaking to them in words that were too simple, too direct, too uncompromising to be acceptable. It is not given to men of compromise to understand parables, for as Herakleitos remarked: "When the things that are right in front of them are pointed out to them, they do not pay attention, though they think they do."

This is the tragedy which most concerns Herakleitos— and which should concern us even more than it did him: the fact that the majority of men think they see, and do not. They believe they listen, but they do not hear. They are "absent when present" because in the act of seeing and hearing they substitute the clichés of familiar prejudice for the new and unexpected truth that is being offered to them. They complacently imagine they are receiving a new light, but in the very moment of apprehension they renew their obsession with the old darkness, which is so familiar that it, and it alone, appears to them to be light.

(BOT 84–85)

From "Letter to an Innocent Bystander," 1960

THE VERY DIFFICULTY of our position comes from the fact that every definite program is now a deception, every precise plan is a trap, every easy solution is intellectual suicide. And that is why we are caught on the horns of a dilemma: whether we "act" or not we are likely to be destroyed. There is a certain innocence in not having a solution. There is a certain innocence in a kind of despair: but only if in despair we find salvation. I mean, despair of this world and what is in it. Despair of men and of their plans, in order to hope for the impossible answer that lies beyond our earthly contradictions, and yet can burst into our world and solve them if only there are some who hope in spite of despair.

(BOT 62)

• • •

The true solutions are not those which we force upon life in accordance with our theories, but those which life itself provides for those who dispose themselves to receive the truth. Consequently our task is to dissociate ourselves from all who have theories which promise clear-cut and infallible solutions, and to mistrust all such theories, not in a spirit of negativism and defeat, but rather trusting life itself, and nature, and if you will permit me, God above all. For since man has decided to occupy the place of God he has shown himself to be by far the blindest, and cruelest, and pettiest and most ridiculous of all the false gods. We can call ourselves innocent only if we refuse to forget this, and if we also do everything we can to make others realize it.

(BOT 62–63)

From The Wisdom of the Desert, *1960*

THOSE WHO CAME TO THE DESERT seeking "salvation" asked the elders for a "word" that would help them to find it—a *verbum salutis,* a "word of salvation." The answers were not intended to be general, universal prescriptions. Rather they were originally concrete and precise keys to particular doors that had to be entered, at a given time, by given individuals. Only later, after much repetition and much quotation, did they come to be regarded as common currency. It will help us to understand these sayings better if we remember their practical and, one might say, existential quality. But by the time St. Benedict in his Rule prescribed that the "Words of the Fathers" were to be read aloud frequently before Compline, they were traditional monastic lore.

(WOD 12–13)

• • •

A certain brother came, once, to Abbot Theodore of Pherme and spent three days begging him to let him hear a word. The Abbot however did not answer him, and he went off sad. So a disciple said to Abbot Theodore: Father, why did you not speak to him? Now he has gone off sad! The elder replied: Believe me, I spoke no word to him because he is a trader in words, and seeks to glory in the words of another.

(WOD 34–35)

• • •

A certain Philosopher asked St. Anthony: Father, how can you be so happy when you are deprived of the consolation of books? Anthony replied: My book, O philosopher, is the nature of created things, and any time I want to read the words of God, the book is before me.

(WOD 62)

• • •

Theophilus of holy memory, Bishop of Alexandria, journeyed to Scete, and the brethren coming together said to

Abbot Pambo: Say a word or two to the Bishop, that his soul may be edified in this place. The elder replied: If he is not edified by my silence, there is no hope that he will be edified by my words.

(WOD 73–74)

From "Theology of Creativity," September–December 1960

WE MUST BEGIN by facing the ambivalence which makes so much of our talk about creativity absurd because it is fundamentally insincere. Why insincere? Because it is so glib, so all-embracing. The popular use of the word creativity is so facile that one feels immediately that it is a pure evasion. It is a trick to avoid thought, and to avoid real communication. When everything is "creative," nothing is creative. But nowadays everything is called creative: we have creative salesmanship, meaning probably obnoxiously aggressive and vulgar salesmanship. We have creative advertising, which is merely outrageously whimsical or arbitrary. We have creative ways of doing everything under the sun, and in every case what is called "creative" is not even more original than what it is supposed to supersede: it implies nothing but a more ponderously stupid emphasis on what is already too familiar. In a word, being "creative" seems to mean little more than rushing forward with breakneck impetuosity into the conventional, the vulgar, or the absurd.

But there is a more serious complaint against our obsession with creativity. The inanity of the popular, commercialized degradation of this concept is merely an innocent "cover" for its self-contradictions when it is used on a deeper level. And here we come face-to-face with the implication of guilt.

The term "creativity" may be seen, if we observe carefully how it is used, to be in some cases nothing less than a justification of destructiveness. It is a negation, an unmaking, justified by a positive-sounding name: "creation." There are, admittedly, almost infinitely interesting possibilities in broken pieces of machinery, ruined houses, even the smashed bodies of human beings. The revelation of these grim but arresting qualities in horrifying objects, contemplated from a certain detached viewpoint, is in fact a positive aesthetic value, and all the more positive by its implied contrast with empty and formalistic attempts at conventional "beauty." Nevertheless, it should be clear that to take delight in a symbolic, or represented, destruction is not far removed from taking delight in actual destruction. The artist may have a perfect right, perhaps even a duty, to protest as effectively and as vocally as he can against man's present state of alienation in a world that seems to be without meaning because of the moral, cultural, and economic crises of society. This protest certainly can be creative, and there is no doubt that it can bring forth great and living art. But when the protest has so taken possession of the artist that he is no longer articulate, and can only express it by gestures equivalent to dashing his brains out against the wall, then there is no longer a question of creativity. What we have is destruction. It may be terribly pitiable, it may be a matter of urgent importance, but creativity is just not the honest word for tongue-tied frustration, helplessness, and self-hate. This means that not every expression of frustration and despair is creative, only such as are really articulate.

(LE 359–60)

• • •

Our misuse of the word and concept of creativity has robbed us of a standard of judgment. We can no longer tell when an artist is expressing something human or merely screaming: we do not even try to interpret the noise, we just react to it one way or another, believing that the mere fact of having a reaction is somehow "creative." One reason for this seems to be that we have begun, out of resentment, to dissociate the creative from the human. We now tend to assume that a humanistic outlook frustrates the real creative urge, which is in some way subhuman, or even antihuman. But this makes our "creativity" nothing more than a destructive and negative reaction against that very element of life and spirit upon which true creativity depends.

At this point, though a partisan declaration is really not called for, it is necessary to make a personal statement in regard to modern art movements, including those that are most experimental and extreme. I want to say quite clearly and emphatically that I am for the people who experiment in modern art. I have in other places and contexts made known my admiration for Picasso, Matisse, Rouault, etc. In this I share the taste of my time and society. I do not intend to call into question the "creativity" of such great artists, though I must admit that the traditional, classic art of the past, especially primitive Italian, Byzantine, and Oriental sacred art, seem to me to be vastly more important and significant. I am interested in abstract art, surrealism, fauvism, action painting, and all the rest. It seems to me that the men who experiment in action painting have every right to do what they are doing, and that they have a claim upon our respectful attention, though I do not believe the publicity and money they receive are in proportion to their so far slight achievements. And though I am persuaded that they have every right to do what they are doing, I find it hard to get very excited about the results. Most action painting is to me little more than a pleasantly intriguing accident, no more worthy of insult than of praise. It is what it is. Comment on it would be absurd, and I suppose that is why the enormous amount of favorable comment that is actually made is couched in peculiarly earnest double-talk which, if it were worth interpreting, would probably turn out to mean nothing whatever. Or perhaps it is simply a justification of its own meaninglessness.

(LE 356–57)

· · ·

For Tillich, the only valid way out for the artist is to face squarely the very anxiety and meaninglessness inherent in contemporary technological culture and "live creatively, expressing the predicament of the most sensitive people of our time in cultural production." A valid religious art in our time will then be a "creative expression of destructive trends." This is a sound justification of modern art when it is the expression of humility and anguish, not of pride and revolt. It is precisely pride that prevents modern man from achieving depth, even when he most seeks it.

(LE 362)

· · ·

The Zen artist does not "study Zen in order to paint." He does not, as is sometimes thought, practice meditation as a means to artistic experience and expression. Zen meditation is not a preliminary step to artistic creation. Indeed the Zen man does not strictly speaking practice meditation at all, in any sense familiar to us in the West. Rather he enters into a purifying struggle against conceptual knowledge, in which he "sweats out" his attachment to images, ideas, symbols, metaphors, analytic judgments, etc., as means for grasping, appreciating, and understanding reality. Instead of this, he seeks to recover an immediate, direct intuition: not so much an intuition "of" being as an intuition which is rooted in and identified with his very existence: an intuition in which the existent knows existence, or "isness," while completely losing sight of itself as a "knowing subject."

In the case of a Zen artist, there is then no artistic reflection. The work of art springs "out of emptiness" and is transferred in a flash, by a few brushstrokes, to paper. It is not a "representation of" anything, but rather it is the subject itself, existing as light, as art, in a drawing which has, so to speak, "drawn itself." The work then is a concretized intuition: not however presented as a unique experience of a specially endowed soul, who can then claim it as his own. On the contrary, to make any such claim would instantly destroy the character of "emptiness" and suchness which the work might be imagined to have. For the Zen man to pretend to share with another "his" experience would be the height of absurdity. Whose experience? Shared with whom? The artist might well be brusquely invited to go home and consider the question: "Who do you think you are, anyway?" I do not know if this question is recorded among the traditional koans, but it deserves to be.

The chief thing about Zen in its relation to art is precisely that the "artist," the "genius as hero," completely vanishes from the scene. There is no self-display, because the "true self," which functions in Zen experience, is empty, invisible, and incapable of being displayed. A disciple once complained to a Zen master that he was unsettled in his mind. The master said: "All right, give me your mind and

I will settle it for you." The disciple's helplessness to pick up his mind and hand it over to somebody else gave him some idea of the nature of his "problems." One cannot begin to be an artist, in Suzuki's sense, until he has become "empty," until he has disappeared.

(LE 363–64)

• • •

Since there is no genuine creativity apart from God, the man who attempts to be a "creator" outside of God and independent of him is forced to fall back on magic. The sin of the wizard is not so much that he usurps and exercises a real preternatural power, but that his postures travesty the divine by degrading man's freedom in absurd and servile manipulations of reality. The dignity of man is to stand before God on his own feet, alive, conscious, alert to the light that has been placed in him, and perfectly obedient to that light. Wizardry and idolatry obscure the light, dim man's vision, and reduce him to a state of infatuated self-absorption in which he plays at unveiling and displaying powers that were meant to remain secret, not in the sense that they must be concealed from others, but in the sense that the artist ought not to be wasting his own attention upon them or calling the attention of others to them. He should be using them in an "empty" and disinterested manner for the good of others and for the glory of God instead of exploiting them to draw attention to himself. The commandment "to make no graven image" is designed first of all to protect man against his inveterate temptation to make gods in his own image, gods in which he can objectify and venerate the divinely given powers he finds in himself. By this magic man seeks to enjoy in himself those powers that were given him as means to find fulfillment beyond and above himself. This bending back upon self, this fixation upon the exterior self was, for St. Augustine, one of the principle elements in the fall of Adam.

(LE 367)

• • •

Man's true creativity is lost, then, with his loss of innocence, selflessness, and simplicity. Oblivious of his external self and empty of self, man was originally one with God his creator. So intimate was their union that the creator could live and act with perfect freedom in his created instrument. Having fallen, and been redeemed in Christ, man is once again able to recover this state of innocence and union, in and through Christ. The Spirit of God, the *Creator Spiritus* who brooded over the waters before the world came into being, dwells in man and broods over the abyss of his human spirit, seeking to call forth from it a new world, a new spiritual creation, in union with the liberty of man redeemed in Christ. The theology of creativity will necessarily be the theology of the Holy Spirit re-forming us in the likeness of Christ, raising us from death to life with the very same power which raised Christ from the dead. The theology of creativity will also be a theology of the image and likeness of God in man. The restoration of our creativity is simply one aspect of our recovery of our likeness to God in Christ. The image of God in man is his freedom, say St. Bernard and St. Gregory of Nyssa. The likeness of God in man is fully restored when man's freedom is perfectly united with the divine freedom, and when, consequently, man acts in all things as God acts. Or rather when God and man act purely and simply as one. Since "God is love" then for man to be restored to the likeness of God, all his acts must

• 43 •

be pure and disinterested love, lacking all taint of that *pro-prium* [common property] which makes him aware of himself as a separate, insecure subject of inordinate needs which he seeks to satisfy at somebody else's expense. Creativity becomes possible insofar as man can forget his limitations and his selfhood and lose himself in abandonment to the immense creative power of a love too great to be seen or comprehended.

(LE 367–68)

• • •

The Christian dimensions of creativity are then to be meditated in the light of such texts as Ephesians 1: 8–10 (the re-establishment of all things in Christ); Colossians 1: 9–29 (the work of God building the Church of saints united in Christ, the "firstborn of every creature," and through him reconciling all things to himself). In this text, particularly, we see the creative role of suffering. This is very important. It is the reply to the secular and demonic overemphasis on the individual, his self-fulfillment in art for its own sake. Here, on the contrary, we see that the cross is the center of the new creation: the tree of life, instead of the tree of the knowledge of good and evil. He who has approached the tree of the knowledge of good and evil has tasted the intoxicating fruit of his own special excellence but he dies the death of frustration. He becomes the prisoner of his own gifts and he sticks to his own excellence as if it were flypaper. There is no joy for him because he is alienated from life, love, and communion in creativity by his own demonic self-assertion, which automatically involves a rejection of suffering, of dependence, of charity, and of obedience.

On the contrary, it is the renunciation of our false self,

the emptying of self in the likeness of Christ, that brings us to the threshold of that true creativity in which God himself, the creator, works in and through us. The fact that the Christian renounces his own limited ends and satisfactions in order to achieve something greater than he can see or understand means the sacrifice of immediate visible results. But it also means that the efficacy of his action becomes lasting as well as universal. Such creativity does not stop with a little ephemeral success here and there: it reaches out to the ends of time and to the limits of the universe.

This may sound like hyperbole: but this is creativity in a new and spiritual dimension, which is its full Christian dimension. And this applies not only to the artist, but to every Christian. To adapt Coomaraswamy's phrase, one might say "the creative Christian is not a special kind of Christian, but every Christian has his own creative work to do, his own part in the mystery of the 'new creation.'" Would that we were all more aware of this. Our awareness would produce a climate that would have a special meaning for the artist. The way for sacred art to become more "creative" is not just for the artist to study new and fashionable trends and try to apply them to sacred or symbolic themes. It is for the artist to enter deeply into his Christian vocation, his part in the work of restoring all things in Christ. But this is not his responsibility alone. This is the responsibility of the whole Church and everybody in it. We all have an obligation to open our eyes to the eschatological dimensions of Christian creativity, for, as St. Paul says, "all creation is groaning" for the final manifestation of this finished work, the only work that has an eternal importance: the full revelation of God by the restoration of all things in Christ.

(LE 369–70)

From a Letter to Napoleón Chow, December 26, 1962

Chow is a Nicaraguan poet and a friend of Ernesto Cardenal and Pablo Antonio Cuadra.

I AM DEFINITELY not a harmonious part of this society: but the fact that I can be considered a part of it at all is testimony to the fact that there does still remain at least a minimum of freedom and the power to speak one's own mind, even though what one says is not always acceptable.

This, it seems to me, is likely to be the place of the Christian writer and intellectual everywhere in the world. I think we have to be very careful of our honesty and our refusal to be swept away by large groups, into monolithic systems. We have to guard and defend our eccentricity, even when we are reminded that it is an expendable luxury, a self-indulgence. It is not, and those who try to make us yield our right to think as we see fit, secretly suffer and are ashamed when we yield to their enticements or to their pressures. Even though they have no other way of praising us than by taking us so seriously that they silence us, this itself is the witness we have to bear to truth.

(CFT 168–69)

From "William Melvin Kelley — The Legend of Tucker Caliban," 1963

THE NEGRO SPIRITUALS of the last century remain as classic examples of what a living liturgical hymnody ought to be, and how it comes into being: not in the study of the research worker or in the monastery library, still less in the halls of Curial offices, but where men suffer oppression, where they are deprived of identity, where their lives are robbed of meaning, and where the desire of freedom and the imperative demand of truth forces them to give it meaning: a religious meaning. Such religion is not the "opium of the people," but a prophetic fire of love and courage, fanned by the breathing of the Spirit of God who speaks to the heart of His children in order to lead them out of bondage.

(LE 168)

From Raids on the Unspeakable, *1966*

WE ARE THE INTELLECTUALS who have taken for granted that we could be "bystanders" and that our quality as detached observers could preserve our innocence and relieve us of responsibility. By intellectual, I do not mean clerk (though I might mean *clerc* [a student or scholar]). I do not mean bureaucrat. I do not mean politician. I do not mean technician. I do not mean anyone whose intelligence ministers to a machine for counting, classifying, and distributing other people: who hands out to this one a higher paycheck and to that one a trip (presently) to the forced labor camp. I do not mean a policeman, or a propagandist. I still dare to use the word intellectual as if it had a meaning.

(RU 54)

• • •

Have you and I forgotten that our vocation, as innocent by-standers—and the very condition of our terrible innocence—is to do what the child did, and keep on saying the king is naked, at the cost of being condemned criminals? Remember, the child in the tale was the only innocent one:

and because of his innocence, the fault of the others was kept from being criminal, and was nothing worse than foolishness. If the child had not been there, they would all have been madmen, or criminals. It was the child's cry that saved them.

(RU 62)

From "Message to Poets," February 1964

COLLECTIVE LIFE is often organized on the basis of cunning, doubt, and guilt. True solidarity is destroyed by the political art of pitting one man against another and the commercial art of estimating all men at a price. On these illusory measurements men build a world of arbitrary values without life and meaning, full of sterile agitation. To set one man against another, one life against another, one work against another, and to express the measurement in terms of cost or of economic privilege and moral honor is to infect everybody with the deepest metaphysical doubt. Divided and set up against one another for the purpose of evaluation, men immediately acquire the mentality of objects for sale in a slave market. They despair of themselves because they know they have been unfaithful to life and to being, and they no longer find anyone to forgive the infidelity.

Yet their despair condemns them to further infidelity: alienated from their own spiritual roots, they contrive to break, to humiliate, and to destroy the spirit of others. In such a situation there is no joy, only rage. Each man feels the deepest root of his being poisoned by suspicion, unbelief, and hate. Each man experiences his very existence as guilt and betrayal, and as a possibility of death: nothing more.

We stand together to denounce the shame and the imposture of all such calculations.

If we are to remain united against these falsehoods, against all power that poisons man and subjects him to the mystifications of bureaucracy, commerce, and the police state, we must refuse the price tag. We must refuse academic classification. We must reject the seductions of publicity.

What characterizes our century is not so much that we have to rebuild our world as that we have to rethink it. This amounts to saying that we have to give it back its language. . . . The vocabularies that are proposed to us are of no use to us . . . and there is no point in a Byzantine exercise upon themes of grammar. We need a profound questioning which will not separate us from the sufferings of men.

(LE 372)

From Conjectures
of a Guilty Bystander, *1966*

THIS IS NO LONGER a time of systematic ethical speculation, for such speculation implies time to reason, and the power to bring social and individual action under the concerted control of reasoned principles upon which most men agree. There is no time to reason out, calmly and objectively, the moral implications of technical developments which are perhaps already superseded by the time one knows enough to reason about them.

Action is not governed by moral reason but by political expediency and the demands of technology—translated into the simple abstract formulas of propaganda. These formulas have nothing to do with reasoned moral action, even though they may appeal to apparent moral values—
—they simply condition the mass of men to react in a desired way to certain stimuli.

Men do not agree in moral reasoning. They concur in the emotional use of slogans and political formulas. There is no persuasion but that of power, of quantity, of pressure, of fear, of desire. Such is our present condition—and it is critical!

(CGB 56–57)

• • •

In a world cluttered and programmed with an infinity of practical signs and consequential digits referring to business, law, government, and war, one who makes such nondescript marks as these is conscious of a special vocation to be inconsequent, to be outside the sequence, and to remain firmly alien to the program. In effect these writings are decidedly hopeful in their own way insofar as they stand outside all processes of production, marketing, consumption, and destruction, which does not however mean that they cannot be bought. Nevertheless, it is clear that these are not legal marks. Nor are they illegal marks, since as far as law is concerned they are perfectly inconsequent. It is this and this alone which gives them a Christian character (Galatians 5), since they obviously do not fit into any familiar setting of religious symbolism, liturgical or otherwise. But one must perhaps ask himself whether it has not now become timely for a Christian who makes a sign or a mark of some sort to feel free about it, and not consider himself rigidly predetermined to a system of glyphs that have a long cultural standing and are fully consequential, even to the point of seeming entirely relevant in the world of business, law, government, and war.

(CGB 181–82)

From "*Answers on Art and Freedom*," *1965*

I AM ASKED WHETHER or not the artist, writer, poet, is a docile servant of institutions, or whether he can and should work in complete freedom. Stated in these terms the proposition would seem to be deceptively simple. One would mechanically answer that the artist is by his very nature free and autonomous. He can be nobody's slave. There is no problem. Everyone sees the answer. It is even *to the interest of those who control him* to allow the artist his autonomy. The relative freedom that is suddenly granted to a Soviet poet becomes a matter of great importance to the whole world. It tends to make people think more kindly and more hopefully of Soviet Russia. Whereas the poet who rebels completely against conventional Western society (Rimbaud, Baudelaire, the Beats) establishes that society more firmly in its complacent philistinism, he also strengthens its conviction that all artists are by necessity opium fiends and feeds its sense of magnanimity in tolerating such people.

What I mean to say by this is that the enemies of the artist's freedom are those who must profit by his *seeming* to be free, whether or not he is so.

And the artist himself, to the extent that he is dominated by introjected philistine condemnations of his art, pours out his energy and integrity in resisting these tyrannical pressures which come to him from within himself. His art then wastes itself in reaction against the antiart of the society in which he lives (or he cultivates antiart as a protest against the art cult of the society in which he lives).

(LE 375–76)

• • •

1. What is the *use* of art? The artist must serenely defend his right to be completely useless. It is better to produce absolutely no work of art at all than to do what can be cynically "used." Yet anything can be used—even the most truculently abstract paintings. They decorate the offices of corporation presidents who have quickly caught on to the fact that to pay ten thousand dollars for something explicitly "useless" is a demonstration of one's wealth and power—as well as of sophistication.

And tomorrow the abstract paintings will be on the walls of the Commissars.

Works of art can be and are used in many ways, but such uses are beyond the range of this question. "Art" considered as an immanent perfection of the artist's own intelligence is not improved by nonartistic use. Let us set aside the question of a supposed cult of pure art, art for art's sake, etc. Is this an actual problem? I doubt it. Who is to say what poets and artists as a species are thinking and doing? The world is full of poets, novelists, painters, sculptors: they blossom on all the bushes. Who can generalize about them, except perhaps to say that they all tend to start out looking for something that can't be found merely by selling insurance or automobiles.

The problem arises when art ceases to be honest work and becomes instead a way to self-advertisement and success—when the writer or painter uses his art merely to sell himself. (It is an article of faith, in Western society at least, that a poet or painter is by nature "more interesting" than other people and, God knows, everybody wants in the worst way to be interesting!)

(LE 377)

• • •

The artist cannot afford passively to accept, to "reflect," or to celebrate what everybody likes. The artist who subscribes to the commercial slogan that the customer is always right will soon be deserted by everybody. The customer has now been trained to think that the *artist* is always right. Thus we have a new situation in which the artist feels himself obligated to function as a prophet or a magician. He sees that he has to be disconcerting, even offensive. Who will ever read him or buy him unless he occasionally insults the customer and all he believes in? That is precisely what the customer wants. He has delegated to the artist the task of nonconforming on his behalf—the task of not conforming with "ordinary decent people." Where does the artist go from there? In desperation he paints a meticulously accurate portrait of a beer can.

(LE 377)

• • •

Certainly the artist has no obligation to promulgate ethical lessons any more than political or economic ones. The artist is not a catechist. Usually moral directives are lost when one attempts to convey them in a medium that is not intended to communicate conceptual formulas. But the artist has a moral obligation to maintain his own freedom and his own truth. His art and his life are separable only in theory. The artist cannot be free in his art if he does not have a conscience that warns him when he is acting like a slave in his everyday life.

The artist should preach nothing—not even his own autonomy. His art should speak its own truth, and in so doing it will be in harmony with every other kind of truth—moral, metaphysical, and mystical.

The artist has no moral obligation to prove himself one of the elect by systematically standing a traditional moral code on its head.

(LE 378)

• • •

Is the artist necessarily committed to this or that political ideology? No. But he does live in a world where politics are decisive and where political power can destroy his art as well as his life. Hence he is indirectly committed to seek some political solution to problems that endanger the freedom of man. This is the great temptation: there is not a single form of government or social system today that does not in the end seek to manipulate or to coerce the artist in one way or another. In every case the artist should be in complete solidarity with those who are fighting for rights and freedom against inertia, hypocrisy, and coercion: e.g., the Negroes in the United States.

(LE 378)

• • •

Society benefits when the artist liberates himself from its coercive or seductive pressures. Only when he is obligated to his fellow man in the concrete, rather than to society in the abstract, can the artist have anything to say that will be of value to others. His art then becomes accidentally a work of love and justice. The artist would do well, however, not to concern himself too much with "society" in the abstract or with ideal "commitments." This has not always been true. It applies more to our time when "society" is in some confusion. It is conceivable that the artist might once again be completely integrated in society as he was in the Middle Ages. Today he is hardly likely to find himself unless he is a nonconformist and a rebel. To say this is neither dangerous nor new. It is what society really expects of its artists. For today the artist has, whether he likes it or not, inherited the combined functions of hermit, pilgrim, prophet, priest, shaman, sorcerer, soothsayer, alchemist, and bonze [a Buddhist monk]. How could such a man be free? How can he really "find himself" if he plays a role that society has predetermined for him? The freedom of the artist is to be sought precisely in the choice of his *work* and not in the choice of the role as "artist" which society asks him to play, for reasons that will always remain very mysterious.

(LE 379)

From the Preface to the Japanese Edition of Thoughts in Solitude, *March 1966*

N O WRITING ON the solitary, meditative dimensions of life can say anything that has not already been said better by the wind in the pine trees. These pages seek nothing more than to echo the silence and peace that is "heard" when the rain wanders freely among the hills and forests. But what can the wind say where there is no hearer? There is then a deeper silence: the silence in which the Hearer is No-Hearer. That deeper silence must be heard before one can speak truly of solitude.

These pages do not attempt to convey any special information, or to answer deep philosophical questions about life. True, they do concern themselves with questions about life. But they certainly do not pretend to do the reader's thinking for him. On the contrary, they invite him to listen for himself. They do not merely speak to him, they remind him that he is a Hearer.

But who is this Hearer?

Beyond the Hearer, is there perhaps No-Hearer?

Who is this No-Hearer?

For such outrageous questions there are no intelligible answers. The only answer is the Hearing itself. The proper climate for such Hearing is solitude.

(HR 111–12)

• • •

If there is no silence beyond and within the many words of doctrine, there is no religion, only a religious ideology. For religion goes beyond words and actions, and attains to the ultimate truth only in silence and Love. Where this silence is lacking, where there are only the "many words" and not the One Word, then there is much bustle and activity, but no peace, no deep thought, no understanding, no inner quiet. Where there is no peace, there is no light and no Love. The mind that is hyperactive seems to itself to be awake and productive, but it is dreaming, driven by fantasy and doubt. One must know how to return to the quiet of worship, the reverent peace of prayer, the adoration in which the entire ego-self silences and abases itself in the presence of the Invisible God to receive His one Word of Love. In these "activities" which are "non-actions" the spirit truly wakes from the dream of a multifarious, confused, and agitated existence. Rooted in non-action, we are ready to act in everything.

Precisely because of this lack, modern Western man is afraid of solitude. He is unable to be alone, to be silent. He is communicating his spiritual and mental sickness to men of the East. Asia is gravely tempted by the violence and activism of the West and is gradually losing hold of its traditional respect for silent wisdom. Therefore it is all the more necessary at this time to rediscover the climate of solitude and of silence; not that everyone can go apart and live alone. But in moments of silence, of meditation, of enlightenment and peace, one learns to be silent and alone everywhere. One learns to lie in the atmosphere of solitude even in the midst of crowds. Not "divided" but one with all in God's Love. For one learns to be a Hearer who is No-Hearer, and one learns to forget all words and listen only to the One Word which seems to be No-Word. One opens the inner door of his heart to the infinite silences of the Spirit out of whose abysses love wells up without fail and gives itself to all. In His silence, the meaning of every sound is finally clear. Only in His silence can the truth of words be distinguished, not in their separateness, but in their pointing to the central unity of Love. All words then say one thing only: that *all is Love.*

(HR 115–16)

From "War and the Crisis of Language," 1967

T HE INCOHERENCE OF LANGUAGE that cannot be trusted and the coherence of weapons that are infallible, or thought to be: this is the dialectic of politics and war, the prose of the twentieth century.

(NVA 235)

· · ·

Now let us turn elsewhere, to the language of advertisement, which at times approaches the mystic and charismatic heights of glossolalia. Here too, utterance is final. No doubt there are insinuations of dialogue, but really there is no dialogue with an advertisement, just as there was no dialogue between the sirens and the crews they lured to disaster on their rocks. There is nothing to do but be hypnotized and drown, unless you have somehow acquired a fortunate case of deafness. But who can guarantee that he is deaf enough? Meanwhile, it is the vocation of the poet—or anti-poet—not to be deaf to such things but to apply his ear intently to their corrupt charms. An example: a perfume advertisement from *The New Yorker* (September 17, 1966).

I present the poem as it appears on a full page, with a picture of a lady swooning with delight at her own smell— the smell of *Arpège*. (Note that the word properly signifies a sound—arpeggio. Aware that we are now smelling music, let us be on our guard!)

> *For the love of Arpège*
> *There's a new hair spray!*
> *The world's most adored fragrance*
> *now in a hair spray. But not hair spray*
> *as you know it.*
>
> *A delicate-as-air-spray*
> *Your hair takes on a shimmer and sheen*
> *that's wonderfully young.*
> *You seem to spray new life and bounce*
> *right into it. And a coif of Arpège has*
> *one more thing no other hair spray has.*
> *It has Arpège.*

One look at this masterpiece and the anti-poet recognizes himself beaten hands down. This is beyond parody. It must stand inviolate in its own victorious rejection of meaning. We must avoid the temptation to dwell on details: interior rhyme, suggestions of an esoteric cult (the use of our product, besides making you young again, is also a kind of gnostic initiation), of magic (our product gives you a hat of smell—a "coif"—it clothes you in an aura of music-radiance-perfume). What I want to point out is the logical *structure* of this sonata: it is a foolproof tautology, locked tight upon itself, impenetrable, unbreakable, irrefutable. It is endowed with a finality so inviolable that it is beyond debate and beyond reason. Faced with the declaration that "Arpège has Arpège," reason is reduced to silence (I almost said despair). Here again we have an example of speech that is at once totally trivial and totally definitive. It has nothing to do with anything real (although of course the sale of the product is a matter of considerable importance to the manufacturer!), but what it says, it says with utter finality.

The unknown poet might protest that he (or she) was not concerned with truth alone but also with beauty—indeed with love. And obviously this too enters into the structure and substance (so to speak) of the text. Just as the argument takes the form of a completely self-enclosed tautological cliché, so the content, the "experience," is one of self-enclosed narcissism woven of misty confusion. It begins with the claim that a new hair spray exists solely for love of itself and yet also exists for love of *you,* baby, because you are somehow subtly identified with Arpège. This perfume is so magic that it not only makes you smell good, it "coifs" you with a new and unassailable identity: it is you who are unassailable because it is you who have somehow become a tautology. And indeed we are reminded that just as Arpège is—or has—Arpège, so, in the popular psychology of women's magazines, "you are eminently lovable because you are just *you.*" When we reflect that the ultimate conceptions of theology and metaphysics have surfaced in such a context—hair spray—we no longer wonder that theologians are tearing their hair and crying that God is dead. After all, when every smell, every taste, every hissing breakfast food is endowed with the transcendental properties of being . . . But let us turn from art, religion, and love to something more serious and more central to the concerns of our time: war.

(NVA 237–38)

•   •   •

The Asian whose future we are about to decide is either a bad guy or a good guy. If he is a bad guy, he obviously has to be killed. If he is a good guy, he is on our side and he ought to be ready to die for freedom. We will provide an opportunity for him to do so: we will kill him to prevent him falling under the tyranny of a demonic enemy. Thus we not only defend his interests together with our own, but we protect his virtue along with our own. Think what might happen if he fell under Communist rule *and liked it!*

The advantages of this kind of logic are no exclusive possession of the United States. This is purely and simply the logic shared by all war-makers. It is the logic of *power.* Possibly American generals are naïve enough to push this logic, without realizing, to absurd conclusions. But all who love power tend to think in some such way. Remember Hitler weeping over the ruins of Warsaw after it had been demolished by the Luftwaffe: "How wicked these people must have been," he sobbed, "to make me do this to them!"

Words like "pacification" and "liberation" have acquired sinister connotations as war has succeeded war. Vietnam has done much to refine and perfect these notions. A "free zone" is now one in which anything that moves is assumed to be "enemy" and can be shot. In order to create a "free zone" that can live up effectively to its name, one must level everything, buildings, vegetation, everything, so that one can clearly see anything that moves, and shoot it. This has very interesting semantic consequences.

(NVA 239)

• • •

So much for the practical language of the battlefield. Let us now attend to the much more pompous and sinister jargon of the war mandarins in government offices and military think-tanks. Here we have a whole community of intellectuals, scholars who spend their time playing out "scenarios" and considering "acceptable levels" in megadeaths. Their language and their thought are as esoteric, as self-enclosed, as tautologous as the advertisement we have just discussed. But instead of being "coifed" in a sweet smell, they are scientifically antiseptic, businesslike, uncontaminated with sentimental concern for life—other than their own. It is the same basic narcissism, but in a masculine, that is, managerial, mode. One proves one's realism along with one's virility by toughness in playing statistically with global death. It is this playing with death, however, that brings into the players' language itself the corruption of death: not physical but mental and moral extinction. And the corruption spreads from their talk, their thinking, to the words and minds of everybody. What happens then is that the political and moral values they claim to be defending are destroyed by the *contempt* that is more and more evident in the language in which they talk about such things. Technological strategy becomes an end in itself and leads the fascinated players into a maze where finally the very purpose strategy was supposed to serve is itself destroyed. The ambiguity of official war talk has one purpose above all: to mask this ultimate unreason and permit the game to go on.

(NVA 240-41)

• • •

Of special importance is the *style* of these nuclear mandarins. The technological puckishness of Herman Kahn is perhaps the classic of this genre. He excels in the sly understatement of the inhuman, the apocalyptic, enormity. His style is esoteric, allusive, yet confidential. The reader has the sense of being a privileged eavesdropper in the councils of the mighty. He knows enough to realize that things are going to happen about which he can do nothing, though perhaps he can save his skin in a properly equipped shelter where he may consider at leisure the rationality of survival in an unlivable world. Meanwhile, the cool tone of the author and the reassuring solemnity of his jargon seem to suggest that those in power, those who turn loose these instruments of destruction, have no intention of perishing themselves, that consequently survival must have a point. The point is not revealed, except that nuclear war is somehow implied to be good business. Nor are H-bombs necessarily a sign of cruel intentions. They enable one to enter into communication with the high priests in the enemy camp. They permit the decision-makers on both sides to engage in a ritual "test of nerve." In any case, the language of escalation is the language of naked power, a language that is all the more persuasive because it is proud of being ethically illiterate and because it accepts, as realistic, the basic irrationality of its own tactics. The language of escalation, in its superb mixture of banality and apocalypse, science and unreason, is the expression of a massive death wish. We can only hope that this death wish is only that of a decaying Western civilization, and that it is not common to the entire race. Yet the language itself is given universal currency by the mass media. It can quickly contaminate the thinking of everybody.

(NVA 241)

• • •

War-makers in the twentieth century have gone far toward creating a political language so obscure, so apt for treachery, so ambiguous, that it can no longer serve as an instrument for peace: it is good only for war. But why? Because the language of the war-maker is *self-enclosed in finality*. It does not invite reasonable dialogue, it uses language to silence dialogue, to block communication, so that instead of words the two sides may trade divisions, positions, villages, air bases, cities—and of course the lives of the people in them. The daily toll of the killed (or the "kill ratio") is perfunctorily scrutinized and decoded. And the totals are expertly managed by "ministers of truth" so that the newspaper reader may get the right message.

Our side is always ahead. He who is winning must be the one who is right. But we are right, therefore we must be winning. Once again we have the beautiful, narcissistic tautology of war—or of advertising. Once again, "Arpège has Arpège." There is no communicating with anyone else, because anyone who does not agree, who is outside the charmed circle, is wrong, is evil, is already in hell.

(NVA 243–44)

• • •

What next? The illness of political language—which is almost universal and is a symptom of a Plague of Power that is common to China and America, Russia and Western Europe—is characterized everywhere by the same sort of double-talk, tautology, ambiguous cliché, self-righteous and doctrinaire pomposity, and pseudoscientific jargon that mask a total callousness and moral insensitivity, indeed a basic contempt for man. The self-enclosed finality that bars all open dialogue and pretends to impose absolute

conditions of one's own choosing upon everybody else ultimately becomes the language of totalitarian dictatorship, if
it is not so already. Revolt against this is taking the form of
another, more elemental and anarchistic, kind of violence,
together with a different semantic code.

(NVA 246–47)

From "Camus and the Church," December 1966

OUR TASK IS NOT suddenly to burst out into the dazzle
of utter unadulterated truth but laboriously to re-
shape an accurate and honest language that will permit
communication between men on all social and intellectual
levels, instead of multiplying a Babel of esoteric and technical tongues which isolate men in their specialities.

(LE 272)

• • •

What characterizes our century is not so much that we
have to rebuild our world as that we have to rethink it.
This amounts to saying that we have to give it back its language. The vocabularies that are proposed to us are of no
use to us and there is no point in a Byzantine exercise upon
themes of grammar. We need a profound questioning
which will not separate us from the sufferings of men.

(LE 272)

• • •

It is unfortunately true that the "Byzantine exercises" not
only of logical positivism (which nevertheless has a certain
limited value) but of all kinds of technical and specialized
thinking tend to remove us from the world in which oth-

ers, and we ourselves, are plunged in the dangers and the sufferings of an increasingly absurd and unmanageable social situation. As Camus and [Brice] Parain[3] have seen, we have to *rethink* that whole situation, and we no longer possess the language with which to do it.

Such a language will necessarily confine itself at first to formulating what is accessible to all men. But it will not talk down to them or cajole them. It will enable them to lift themselves up. Yet if the artist, the peasant, the scientist, and the workman are all going to communicate together, their language will have to have a certain simplicity and austerity in order to be clear to them all without degrading thought. This means not the attainment of a pure classic prose (though Camus admits he thinks of a "new Classicism") but rather of a kind of "superior banality" which will consist in "returning to the words of everybody, but bringing to them the honesty that *is required for them to be purified of lies and hatred.*"

It is at this point that we can see what Camus is asking not only of intellectuals but also of the Church: this *purification and restitution of language so that the truth may become once again unambiguous and fully accessible to all men, especially when they need to know what to do.*

(LE 272–73)

From Cables to the Ace, or Familiar Liturgies of Misunderstanding, *May 1967*

DECODING THE LOOKS OF OPPOSITES. Writing down their silences. Words replaced by moods. Actions punctuated by the hard fall of imperatives. More and more

---

3. Brice Parain was a friend of Albert Camus's who wrote on the phenomenology of language. Parain was an existentialist who became a Catholic in the late 1940s.—Ed.

smoke. Since language has become a medium in which we are totally immersed, there is no longer any need to say anything. The saying says itself all around us. No one need attend. Listening is obsolete. So is silence. Each one travels alone in a small blue capsule of indignation. (Some of the better informed have declared war on language.)

(CP 397)

• • •

"I am doubted, therefore I am. Does this mean that if I insist on making everybody doubt me more, I will become more real? It is enough to doubt them back. By this mutual service we make one another complete. A metaphysic of universal suspicion!" (These words were once heard, uttered by a lonely, disembodied voice, seemingly in a cloud. No one was impressed by them and they were immediately forgotten.)

(CP 400)

From a Letter to Dom Francis Decroix, August 21, 1967

Dom Francis Decroix, abbot of the Cistercian monastery of Frattocchie, near Rome, received a request from Paul VI for a "message of contemplatives to the world." The pope suggested that Thomas Merton might compose the message.

CAN I TELL YOU that I have found answers to the questions that torment the man of our time? I do not know if I have found answers. When I first became a monk, yes, I was more sure of "answers." But as I grow old in the monastic life and advance further into solitude,

I become aware that I have only begun to seek the questions. And what are the questions? Can man make sense out of his existence? Can man honestly give his life meaning merely by adopting a certain set of explanations which pretend to tell him why the world began and where it will end, why there is evil and what is necessary for a good life? My brother, perhaps in my solitude I have become as it were an explorer for you, a searcher in realms which you are not able to visit—except perhaps in the company of your psychiatrist. I have been summoned to explore a desert area of man's heart in which explanations no longer suffice, and in which one learns that only experience counts. An arid, rocky, dark land of the soul, sometimes illuminated by strange fires which men fear and peopled by specters which men studiously avoid except in their nightmares. And in this area I have learned that one cannot truly know hope unless he has found out how like despair hope is. The language of Christianity has said this for centuries in other less naked terms. But the language of Christianity has been so used and so misused that sometimes you distrust it: you do not know whether or not behind the word "Cross" there stands the experience of mercy and salvation, or only the threat of punishment. If my word means anything to you, I can say to you that I have experienced the Cross to mean mercy and not cruelty, truth and not deception: that the news of the truth and love of Jesus is indeed the true good news, but in our time it speaks out in strange places. And perhaps it speaks out in you more than it does in me: perhaps Christ is nearer to you than He is to me: this I say without shame or guilt because I have learned to rejoice that Jesus is in the world in people who know Him not, that He is at work in them when they think themselves far from Him, and it is my joy to tell you to hope though you think that for you of all men hope is impossible. Hope not because you think you can be good, but because God loves us irrespective of our merits and whatever is good in us comes from His love, not from our own doing. Hope because Jesus is with those who are poor and outcasts and perhaps despised even by those who should seek them and care for them most lovingly because they act in God's name.

(HGL 156–57)

From "Baptism in the Forest: Wisdom and Initiation in William Faulkner," 1967

WISDOM IS NOT ONLY SPECULATIVE, but also practical: that is to say, it is "lived." And unless one "lives" it, one cannot "have" it. It is not only speculative but creative. It is expressed in living signs and symbols. It proceeds, then, not merely from knowledge *about* ultimate values, but from an actual possession and awareness of these values as incorporated in one's own existence.

But *sapientia* is not inborn. True, the seeds of it are there, but they must be cultivated. Hence wisdom develops not by itself but in a hard discipline of traditional training, under the expert guidance of one who himself possesses it and who therefore is qualified to teach it. For wisdom cannot be learned from a book. It is acquired only in a living formation; and it is tested by the master himself in certain critical situations.

I might say at once that creative writing and imaginative criticism provide a privileged area for wisdom in the modern world. At times one feels they do so even more than current philosophy and theology. The literary and creative current of thought that has been enriched and stimulated by depth psychology, comparative religion, social anthropology, existentialism, and the renewal of classical, patristic, Biblical, and mystical studies has brought in a sapiential harvest which is not to be despised.

(LE 99)

. . .

What is the position of a believing Christian before the sick and bewildering gnosticism of modern literature? First of all, while respecting the truth and accuracy of his own religious belief, the Christian realizes that today he lives in a world where most people find Christian doctrine incomprehensible or irrelevant. Most modern literature speaks a language that is neither Christian nor unchristian. It seeks to explore reality in terms that are often symbolic, mythical, sapiential, vaguely religious. The modern reader is intolerant of dogmatism, whether it be Christian, Marxist, behaviorist, or any other; and he demands of the novelist, the dramatist, and the poet that they seek their own kind of revelation. The present book is a sympathetic and reasonable survey in which scholars of varying beliefs and viewpoints have joined to explore this area in literature. Their studies show us that what we find in modern literature, when we find any religious wisdom at all, is not a coherent intellectual view of life but a creative effort to penetrate the meaning of man's suffering and aspirations in symbols that are imaginatively authentic. If God does appear in such symbols, we can expect to find Him expressed negatively and obscurely rather than with the positive and rewarding effulgence that we find in the poetry of other ages.

No sense can be made of modern literature if we are not willing to accept the fact that we live in an age of doubt. But even in the midst of this doubt we can find authentic assurances of hope and understanding, provided that we are willing to tolerate theological discomfort. Derek Stanford's quotation from Dylan Thomas sums up the casual but unimpeachable sincerity of modern sapiential literature:

"These poems, with all their crudities, doubts, and confusions, are written for the love of Man and in praise of God, and I'd be a damn' fool if they weren't."

(LE 115)

From "Auschwitz, a Family Camp," circa 1967

L ANGUAGE ITSELF HAS FALLEN VICTIM to total war, genocide, and systematic tyranny in our time. In destroying human beings, and human values, on a mass scale, the Gestapo also subjected the German language to violence and crude perversion.

. . . The language of Auschwitz is one of the vulnerable spots through which we get a clear view of the demonic.

Gestapo double-talk encircles reality as a doughnut encircles its hole. "Special treatment," "special housing." We need no more than one lesson, and we gain the intuition which identifies the hole, the void of death, in the heart of the expression. When the circumlocution becomes a little more insistent ("recovery camps for the tired") it brings with it suggestions of awful lassitude, infinite hopelessness, as if meaning had now been abolished forever and we were definitively at the mercy of the absurd.

"Disinfectants," "materials for resettlement of Jews," "Ovaltine substitute from Swiss Red Cross"—all references to Zyklon B! When a deadly poison gas is referred to as a soothing restorative, a quasi-medicine to put babies to sleep, one senses behind the phrase a deep hatred of life itself. The key to Auschwitz language is its pathological joy in death. This turns out to be the key to all officialese. All of it is the celebration of boredom, of routine, of deadness, of organized futility. Auschwitz just carried the whole thing to its logical extreme, with a kind of heavy lilt in its mockery, its oafish love of death.

"Work makes free"—the sign over the gate of Auschwitz—tells, with grim satisfaction, the awful literal truth: "Here we work people to death." And behind it the dreadful metaphysical admission: "For us there is only one freedom, death."

"To the Bath," said the sign pointing to the gas chambers. (You will be purified of that dirty thing, your life!) And as a matter of fact the gas chambers and crematories were kept spotlessly clean. "Nothing was left of them [the victims], not even a speck of dust on the armatures."

"Assigned to harvest duty"—this, in the record of an SS man, meant he had been posted to Auschwitz. The double meaning of "harvest" was doubtless not random. It has an apocalyptic ring.

(NVA 155–56)

From "Why Alienation Is for Everybody," 1968

I F WE WANT TO UNDERSTAND alienation we have to find where its deepest taproot goes—and we have to realize that this root will always be there. Alienation is inseparable from culture, from civilization, and from life in society. It is not just a feature of "bad" cultures, "corrupt" civilizations, or urban society. It is not just a dubious privilege reserved for some people in society. In Louisville, it is not just for the West End. In my opinion the East End may be even more alienated than the West because it is not aware of the fact.

Alienation begins when culture divides me against myself, puts a mask on me, gives me a role I may or may not want to play. Alienation is complete when I become completely identified with my mask, totally satisfied with my role, and convince myself that any other identity or role is inconceivable. The man who sweats under his mask, whose role makes him itch with discomfort, who hates the division in himself, is already beginning to be free. But God help him if all he wants is the mask the other man is wearing, just because the other one does not seem to be sweating or itching. Maybe he is no longer human enough to itch. (Or else he pays a psychiatrist to scratch him.)

(LE 381)

• • •

Modern literature is by and large a literature of alienation, not only because we are painfully living through the collapse of a culture but because today we have more culture and more civilization than we know what to do with. There are not only the simple, beautiful, wild, honest ceremonial masks once affected by the Kwakiutl Indians (and which were well understood because they had their "right" place in life and went with some pretty good dancing): but today we smother under an overproduction of masks and myths and personae. We all have to try to be fifty different people. We all can refuse some of the more absurd and unacceptable roles, but not many can refuse as much as they would like to, and no one can refuse them all.

The result is the painful, sometimes paranoid sense of being always under observation, under judgment, for not fulfilling some role or other we have forgotten we were supposed to fulfill.

The peculiar pain of "alienation" in its ordinary sense —alienation as a kind of perpetual mental Charley horse of self-conscious frustration—is that nobody really has to look at us or judge us or despise us or hate us. Whether or not they do us this service, we are already there ahead of them. We are doing it for them. WE TRAIN OUR-SELVES OBEDIENTLY TO HATE OURSELVES SO MUCH THAT OUR ENEMIES NO LONGER HAVE TO. To live in constant awareness of this bind is a kind of living death. But to live without any awareness of it at all is death pure and simple—even though one may still be walking around and smelling perfect.

(LE 381–82)

. . .

The best cultures have always been those which achieved the most workable balance between custom and nature, discipline and impulse, conscious and unconscious. Primitive cultures on the whole did this well. The great traditional religious cultures managed it well (Mayan, Zapotecan, the Buddhist-inspired Kingdom of Asoka, some medieval Christian cultures). Our culture is doing a disastrously bad job of it.

What can the artist do about it?

It is not enough to complain about alienation, one must exorcise it. One must refuse the most useless and harmful role it imposes on us: that of causing and judging our own pain and condemning ourselves to nonentity on account of it. The constant, repeated, compulsive self-annihilation is due to the short circuit which puts a conventional judgment, dictated by culture, fashion, literature, style, art, religion, science, sociology, politics, what have you, IN THE PLACE OF OUR OWN IMMEDIATE RESPONSE however unconscious, irrational, foolish, unacceptable, it may at first appear to be. (Immediate response is not "knee-jerk" response, and it does imply some cultural formation and experience.)

Yes, we have to learn to write disciplined prose. We have to write poems that are "Poems." But that is a relatively unprofitable and secondary concern compared with the duty of first writing nonsense. We have to learn the knack of free association, to let loose what is hidden in our depths, to expand rather than to condense prematurely. Rather than making an intellectual point and then devising a form to express it, we need rather to release the face that is sweating under the mask and let it sweat out in the open for a change, even though nobody else gives it a prize for special beauty or significance.

(LE 383–84)

From "Monastic Experience and East-West Dialogue," 1968

The following text is from notes for a paper that was to have been delivered in Calcutta in October 1968.

1. IN ALL THE GREAT WORLD RELIGIONS there are a few individuals and communities who dedicate themselves in a special way to living out the full consequences and implications of what they believe. This dedication may take a variety of forms, some temporary, some permanent; some active and some intellectual; some ascetic, contemplative, and mystical. In this paper the term "monastic" is applied in a broad way to those forms of special contemplative dedication which include:

(a) A certain distance or detachment from the "ordinary" and "secular" concerns of worldly life; a monastic solitude, whether partial or total, temporary or permanent.

(b) A preoccupation with the radical inner depth of one's religious and philosophical beliefs, the inner and experimental "ground" of those beliefs, and their outstanding spiritual implications.

(c) A special concern with inner transformation, a deepening of consciousness toward an eventual breakthrough and discovery of a transcendent dimension of life beyond that. We can see the point of sharing in those disciplines which claim to prepare a way for "mystical" self-transcendence (with due reservations in the use of the term "mystical").

(AJ 309)

• • •

I speak as a Western monk who is pre-eminently concerned with his own monastic calling and dedication. I have left my monastery to come here not just as a research scholar or even as an author (which I also happen to be). I come as a pilgrim who is anxious to obtain not just information, not just "facts" about other monastic traditions, but to drink from ancient sources of monastic vision and experience. I seek not only to learn more (quantitatively) about religion and about monastic life, but to become a better and more enlightened monk (qualitatively) myself.

I am convinced that communication in depth, across the lines that have hitherto divided religious and monastic traditions, is now not only possible and desirable, but most important for the destinies of Twentieth-Century Man.

I do not mean that we ought to expect visible results of earthshaking importance, or that any publicity at all is desirable. On the contrary, I am convinced that this exchange must take place under the true monastic conditions of quiet, tranquility, sobriety, leisureliness, reverence, meditation, and cloistered peace. I am convinced that what one might call typically "Asian" conditions of non-hurrying and of patient waiting must prevail over the Western passion for immediate visible results. For this reason I think it is above all important for Westerners like myself to learn what little they can from Asia, *in* Asia. I think we must seek not merely to make superficial reports *about* the Asian traditions, but to live and share those traditions, as far as we can, by living them in their traditional milieu.

(AJ 312–13)

• • •

True communication on the deepest level is more than a simple sharing of ideas, of conceptual knowledge, or formulated truth. The kind of communication that is necessary on this deep level must also be "communion" beyond the level of words, a communion in authentic experience which is shared not only on a "preverbal" level but also on a "post-verbal" level.

The "preverbal" level is that of the unspoken and indefinable "preparation," "the predisposition" of mind and heart, necessary for all "monastic" experience whatever. This demands among other things a "freedom from automatisms and routines," and candid liberation from external social dictates, from conventions, limitations, and mechanisms which restrict understanding and inhibit experience of the new, the unexpected. Monastic training must not form men in a rigid mold, but liberate them from habitual and routine mechanisms. The monk who is to communicate on the level that interests us here must be not merely a punctilious observer of external traditions, but a living example of traditional and interior realization. He must be wide open to life and to new experience because he has fully utilized his own tradition and gone beyond it.

This will permit him to meet a discipline of another, apparently remote and alien tradition, and find a common ground of verbal understanding with him. The "post-verbal" level will then, at least ideally, be that on which they both meet beyond their own words and their own understanding in the silence of an ultimate experience which might conceivably not have occurred if they had not met and spoken. This I would call "communion." I think it is something that the deepest ground of our being cries out for, and it is something for which a lifetime of striving would not be enough.

(AJ 315–16)

From an Informal Talk Delivered in Calcutta, October 1968

A RE MONKS AND HIPPIES and poets relevant? No, we are deliberately irrelevant. We live with an ingrained irrelevance which is proper to every human being. The marginal man accepts the basic irrelevance of the human condition, an irrelevance which is manifested above all by the fact of death. The marginal person, the monk, the displaced person, the prisoner, all these people live in the presence of death, which calls into question the meaning of life. He struggles with the fact of death in himself, trying to seek something deeper than death; because there is something deeper than death, and the office of the monk or the marginal person, the meditative person or the poet is to go beyond death even in this life, to go beyond the dichotomy of life and death and to be, therefore, a witness to life.

(AJ 306)

●　●　●

And so I stand among you as one who offers a small message of hope, that first, there are always people who dare to seek on the margin of society, who are not dependent on social acceptance, not dependent on social routine, and prefer a kind of free-floating existence under a state of risk. And among these people, if they are faithful to their own calling, to their own vocation, and to their own message from God, communication on the deepest level is possible.

And the deepest level of communication is not communication, but communion. It is wordless. It is beyond words, and it is beyond speech, and it is beyond concept. Not that we discover a new unity. We discover an older unity. My dear brothers, we are already one. But we imagine that we are not. And what we have to recover is our original unity. What we have to be is what we are.

(AJ 307–8)

• • •

The following text is from Merton's last talk, "Marxism and Monastic Perspectives," delivered on the day he died by accidental electrocution, December 10, 1968.

THE MONK IS A MAN who has attained, or is about to attain, or seeks to attain, full realization. He dwells in the center of society as one who has attained realization—he knows the score. Not that he has acquired unusual or esoteric information, but he has come to experience the ground of his own being in such a way that he knows the secret of liberation and can somehow or other communicate this to others.

Now, in patristic doctrine and in the teaching of the monastic fathers, you find this very strongly stressed. You find, for example, the Cistercians of the 12th century speaking of a kind of monastic therapy. Adam of Perseigne has the idea that you come to the monastery, first, to be cured. The period of monastic formation is a period of cure, of convalescence. When one makes one's profession, one has passed through convalescence and is ready to begin to be educated in a new way—the education of the "new man." The whole purpose of the monastic life is to teach men to live by love.

The simple formula, which was so popular in the West, was the Augustinian formula of the translation of *cupiditas* into *caritas,* of self-centered love into an outgoing, other-centered love. In the process of this change the individual ego was seen to be illusory and dissolved itself, and in place of this self-centered ego came the Christian person, who was no longer just the individual but was Christ dwelling in each one. So in each one of us the Christian person is that which is fully open to all other persons, because ultimately all other persons are Christ.

(AJ 333–34)

On Poetry

Journal Entry, October 1, 1939

WHEN BLAKE SAID some of his work was dictated by angels he did not mean that, because all other poetry was merely written by men, his was superior to theirs. On the contrary he meant that all good poetry was "dictated by angels" and that he himself could not claim any praise for "his" verses. They were not really his.

But nowadays, since men are supposed to be the highest of *all* creatures, because they are at the top of the ladder of evolution, we are very careful to guard that position against anything higher—angels—God. To presume that poetry could be dictated by a creature higher than man, then, seems an affront: and since angels are only "symbols," Blake seemed to be speaking by symbols to say he was the greatest of poets. But his statement was not one of pride but one of humility, because, as it happened, he believed in angels.

The only thing he meant was, he was at least a poet, while other writers, to whom the angels did not dictate (Klopstock, for example) were not poets. But to be a poet and not to recognize it would be a false humility: the only humility a poet is not allowed. The poet's humility is to write "in fear and trembling" (as he said to Samuel Palmer, if I have the reference right) and that he must.

(RUN 36–37)

Journal Entry, October 1, 1941

SUPPOSING ANYBODY were to be so rash as to ask why there aren't any good poets among American Catholics today: what would be the real answer, besides the loud mockery of everybody who ever read a true poet?

Why is it that modern Catholic poets in America are, of all groups, perhaps the most trivial and the most common-place, not even saved by the fact that they are well-disposed towards God, and intend, sometimes, to praise Him? We are worse poets than the liberals and the communists even, and that is going far! They are worse than all the surreal-ists, who are mostly phony and frantic and diabolical and crazy, and yet sometimes knock you out of your chair with a good line. They are worse than all the accepted, and not *too* blameworthy, corn-belt people, American scene fel-lows, who are, at worst, pompous and boring!

What is one thing all poets need to know? They need to be reminded of their nearness to the Saints, just as everybody has to be reminded of this. To do anything any good in the world, you have to renounce the world in order to do that thing: you have to love it and give it your whole life. . . .

The reason there are so few good Catholic poets is the same as the reason why there are so few Catholics, of the educated classes, anyway, that have really shown a great desire for saintliness—we are all mediocre, indifferent, concerned with trivialities, or small questions of pride, or are drawn into various political traps: many men of good intentions are trapped into Fascism, because they think they can serve God with political crusades before they have given everything to the poor and taken up their spiritual crosses of poverty and humiliation before men! And after they have done that, no military crusade makes too much sense, if it is predominantly a crusade, and an offensive!

(RUN 419–20)

From "The Poet, to His Book," 1948

Now is the day of our farewell in fear, lean
    pages:
And shall I leave some blessing on the half of
    me you have devoured?
Were you, in clean obedience, my Cross,
Sent to exchange my life for Christ's in labor?
How shall the seeds upon those furrowed
    papers flower?
Or have I only bled to sow you full of stones
    and thorns,
Feeding my minutes to my own dead will?

Or will your little shadow fatten in my life's last
    hour
And darken for a space my gate to white
    eternity?

And will I wear you once again, in Purgatory,
Around my mad ribs like a shirt of flame?
Or bear you on my shoulders for a sorry jubilee
My Sinbad's burden?

Is that the way you'd make me both-ways' loser,
Paying the prayers and joys you stole of me,
You thirsty traitor, in my Trappist mornings!

Go, stubborn talker,
Find you a station on the loud world's corners,
And try there, (if your hands be clean) your
    length of patience:
Use there the rhythms that upset my silences,
And spend your pennyworth of prayer
There in the clamor of the Christless avenues:

And try to ransom some one prisoner
Out of those walls of traffic, out of the wheels of
    that unhappiness!

(CP 192–93)

From "Poetry, Symbolism, and Typology," 1953

THE PSALMS ARE POEMS, and poems have a meaning—although the poet has no obligation to make his meaning immediately clear to anyone who does not want to make an effort to discover it. But to say that poems have meaning is not to say that they must necessarily convey practical information or an explicit message. In poetry, words are charged with meaning in a far different way than are the words in a piece of scientific prose. The words of a poem are not merely the signs of concepts: they are also rich in affective and spiritual associations. The poet uses words not merely to make declarations, statements of fact. That is usually the last thing that concerns him. He seeks above all to put words together in such a way that they exercise a mysterious and vital reactivity among themselves, and so release their secret content of associations to produce in the reader an experience that enriches the depths of his spirit in a manner quite unique. A good poem induces an experience that could not be produced by any other combination of words. It is therefore an entity that stands by itself, graced with an individuality that marks it off from every other work of art. Like all great works of art, true poems seem to live by a life entirely their own. What we must seek in a poem is therefore not an accidental reference to something outside itself: we must seek this inner principle of individuality and of life which is its soul, or "form." What the poem actually "means" can only be summed up in the whole content of poetic experience which it is capable of producing in the reader. This total poetic experience is what the poet is trying to communicate to the rest of the world.

(LE 327)

• • •

Light and darkness, sun and moon, stars and planets, trees, beasts, whales, fishes, and birds of the air, all these things in the world around us and the whole natural economy in which they have their place have impressed themselves upon the spirit of man in such a way that they naturally tend to mean to him much more than they mean in themselves. That is why, for example, they enter so mysteriously into the substance of our poetry, of our visions, and of our dreams. That too is why an age, like the one we live in, in which cosmic symbolism has been almost forgotten and submerged under a tidal wave of trademarks, political party buttons, advertising and propaganda slogans, and all the rest—is necessarily an age of mass psychosis. A world in which the poet can find practically no material in the common substance of everyday life, and in which he is driven crazy in his search for the vital symbols that have been buried alive under a mountain of cultural garbage, can only end up, like ours, in self-destruction. And that is why some of the best poets of our time are running wild among the tombs in the moonlit cemeteries of surrealism. Faithful to the instincts of the true poet, they are unable to seek their symbols anywhere save in the depths of the spirit where these symbols are found. These depths have become a ruin and a slum. But poetry must, and does, make good use of whatever it finds there: starvation, madness, frustration, and death.

(LE 333)

From "Poetry and Contemplation: A Reappraisal," October 24, 1958

THE CHRISTIAN'S VISION of the world ought, by its very nature, to have in it something of poetic inspiration. Our faith ought to be capable of filling our hearts with a wonder and a wisdom which see beyond the surface of things and events, and grasp something of the inner and "sacred" meaning of the cosmos which, in all its movements and all its aspects, sings the praises of its Creator and Redeemer.

No Christian poetry worthy of the name has been written by anyone who was not in some degree a contemplative. I say "in some degree" because obviously not all Christian poets are mystics. But the true poet is always akin to the mystic because of the "prophetic" intuition by which he sees the spiritual reality, the inner meaning of the object he contemplates, which makes that concrete reality not only a thing worthy of admiration in itself, but also and above all makes it a *sign of God.* All good Christian poets are then contemplatives in the sense that they see God everywhere in His creation and in His mysteries, and behold the created world as filled with signs and symbols of God. To the true Christian poet, the whole world and all the incidents of life tend to be sacraments—signs of God, signs of His love working in the world.

However, the mere fact of having this contemplative vision of God in the world around us does not necessarily make a man a great poet. One must be not a "seer" but also and especially a "creator"—a "maker." Poetry is an art, a natural skill, a virtue of the practical intellect, and no matter how great a subject we may have in the experience of contemplation, we will not be able to put it into words if we do not have the proper command of our medium. This is true. But let us assume that a man already has this natural gift. If the inspiration is helpless without a correspondingly effective technique, technique is barren without inspiration.

(LE 345)

• • •

Christ is the inspiration of Christian poetry, and Christ is at the center of the contemplative life. Therefore, it would seem fairly evident that the one thing that will most contribute to the perfection of Catholic literature in general and poetry in particular will be for our writers and poets to live more as "contemplatives" than as citizens of a materialistic world. This means first of all leading the full Christian sacramental and liturgical life insofar as they can in their state. Obviously, the poet does not have to enter a monastery to be a better poet. On the contrary, what we need are "contemplatives" outside the cloister and outside the rigidly fixed patterns of religious life—contemplatives in the world of art, letters, education, and even politics. This means a solid integration of one's work, thought, religion, and family life and recreations in one vital harmonious unity with Christ at its center. The liturgical life is the most obvious example of "active contemplation," but it is hard enough to find a parish where the liturgical life is anything more than a bare skeleton. The eccentricities and obsessions of occasional faddists should not prejudice us against the immense vitality and permanent value of the true liturgical revival. It is quite certain that one of the most valid achievements in the realm of Christian art in our time is to the credit of the monks of Solesmes, with their revival of Gregorian chant.

(LE 345–46)

• • •

A genuine aesthetic experience is something which transcends not only the sensible order (in which, however, it has its beginning) but also that of reason itself. It is a suprarational intuition of the latent perfection of things. Its immediacy outruns the speed of reasoning and leaves all analysis far behind. In the natural order, as Jacques Maritain has often insisted, it is an analogue of the mystical experience which it resembles and imitates from afar. Its mode of apprehension is that of "co-naturality"—it reaches out to grasp the inner reality, the vital substance of its object, by a kind of affective identification of itself with it. It rests in the perfection of things by a kind of union which sometimes resembles the quiescence of the soul in its immediate affective contact with God in the obscurity of mystical prayer. A true artist can contemplate a picture for hours, and it is a real contemplation, too. So close is the resemblance between these two experiences that a poet like Blake could almost confuse the two and make them merge into one another as if they belonged to the same order of things.

(LE 347)

• • •

What, then, is the conclusion? That poetry can, indeed, help to bring us rapidly through that early part of the journey to contemplation that is called active: but when we are entering the realm of true contemplation, where eternal happiness is tasted in anticipation, poetic intuition may ruin our rest in God "beyond all images."

In such an event, one might at first be tempted to say that there is only one course for the poet to take, if he wants to be a mystic or a saint: he must consent to the *ruthless and complete sacrifice of his art.* Such a conclusion would seem to be dictated by logic. If there is an infinite distance between the gifts of nature and those of grace, between the natural and the supernatural order, man and God, then should not one always reject the natural for the supernatural, the temporal for the eternal, the human for the divine? It seems to be so simple as to defy contradiction. And yet, when one has experience in the strange vicissitudes of the inner life, and when one has seen something of the ways of God, one remembers that there is a vast difference between the logic of men and the logic of God. There is indeed no human logic in the ways of interior prayer, only Divine paradox. Our God is not a Platonist. Our Christian spirituality is not the intellectualism of Plotinus or the asceticism of the Stoics. We must therefore be very careful of oversimplifications. The Christian is sanctified not merely by always making the choice of "the most perfect thing." Indeed, experience teaches us that the most perfect choice is not always that which is most perfect in itself. The most perfect choice is *the choice of what God has willed for us,* even though it may be, in itself, less perfect, and indeed less "spiritual."

It is quite true that aesthetic experience is only a temporal thing, and like all other temporal things it passes away. It is true that mystical prayer enriches man a hundredfold in time and in eternity. It purifies the soul and loads it with supernatural merits, enlarging man's powers and capacities to absorb the infinite rivers of divine light which will one day be his beatitude. The sacrifice of art would seem to be a small enough price to lay down for this "pearl of great price."

But let us consider for a moment whether the Christian contemplative poet is necessarily confronted with an absolute clean-cut "either/or" choice between "art" and "mystical prayer."

It can of course happen that a contemplative and artist finds himself in a situation in which he is morally certain that God demands of him the sacrifice of his art, in order that he may enter more deeply into the contemplative life. In such a case, the sacrifice must be made, not because this is a general law binding all artist-contemplatives, but because it is the will of God in this particular, concrete case.

But it may equally well happen that an artist who imagines himself to be called to the higher reaches of mystical prayer is not called to them at all. It becomes evident, to him, that the simplest and most obvious thing for him is to be an artist, and that he should sacrifice his aspirations for a deep mystical life and be content with the lesser gifts with which he has been endowed by God. For such a one, to insist on spending long hours in prayer frustrating his creative instinct would, in fact, lead to illusion. His efforts to be a contemplative would be fruitless. Indeed, he would find that by being an artist—and at the same time living fully all the implications of art for a Christian and for a contemplative in the broad sense of the word—he would enjoy a far deeper and more vital interior life, with a much richer appreciation of the mysteries of God, than if he just tried to bury his artistic talent and be a professional "saint." If he is called to be an artist, then his art will lead him to sanctity, if he uses it as a Christian should.

(LE 352–53)

• • •

We may apply the last words of this text to our present case. If the Christian poet is truly a Christian poet, if he has a vocation to make known to other men the unsearchable mystery of the love of Christ, then he must do so in the Spirit of Christ. And his "manifestation of the Spirit" not only springs from a kind of contemplative intuition of the mystery of Christ, but is "given to him for his profit" and will therefore deepen and perfect his union with Christ. The Christian poet and artist is one who grows not only by his contemplation but also by his open declaration of the mercy of God. If it is clear that he is called to give this witness to God, then he can say with St. Paul: "Woe to me if I preach not the Gospel." At the same time, he should always remember that the hidden and more spiritual gifts are infinitely greater than his art, and if he is called upon to make an exclusive choice of one or the other, he must know how to sacrifice his art.

(LE 354)

From a Letter to Helen Wolff, May 8, 1959

Helen Wolff was the publisher at Pantheon Books, which published Doctor Zhivago *in the United States.*

CERTAINLY I FEEL that the Christian poetry and literature of our time must abandon static and outworn concepts and utter their praise of Christ in intuitions that are dynamic and in full movement. Such is Pasternak's vision of reality, a reality which must be caught as it passes, reality which must carry us away with it. If we pause even for a moment to formulate abstractions we will have lost life as it goes by. *Timeo Jesum transeuntem et non revertentem* (I fear Jesus will go by and will not come back—as St. Augustine says). This is the very vision of reality we have in the *I Ching.*

How great is this cosmic temple of God in which we live, great though blackened by the smoke of our conflicts! Have no anxiety for Kurt. There is a far greater dimension to his life than that which is limited by a few years. Let him walk always with his head in the stars. And all of us the same.

(CFT 97)

From New Seeds of Contemplation, 1961

THE POET ENTERS into himself in order to create. The contemplative enters into God in order to be created.

(NS 111)

• • •

A Catholic poet should be an apostle by being first of all a poet. Not try to be a poet by being first of all an apostle. For if he presents himself to people as a poet, he is going to be judged as a poet and if he is not a good one his apostolate will be ridiculed.

(NS 111)

From "William Melvin Kelley: The Legend of Tucker Caliban," 1963

THE DEEP ELEMENTAL STIRRINGS that lead to social change begin within the hearts of men whose thoughts have hitherto not been articulate or who have never gained a hearing, and whose needs are therefore ignored, suppressed, and treated as if they did not exist. There is no revolution without a voice. The passion of the oppressed must first of all make itself heard at least among themselves, in spite of the insistence of the privileged oppressor that such needs cannot be real, or just, or urgent. The more the cry of the oppressed is ignored, the more it strengthens itself with a mysterious power that is to be gained from myth, symbol, and prophecy. There is no revolution without poets who are also seers. There is no revolution without prophetic songs.

(LE 168)

From "Message to Poets," February 1964

This message was read at a meeting of the "new" Latin-American poets, Mexico City, February 1964.

WE WHO ARE POETS know that the reason for a poem is not discovered until the poem itself exists. The reason for a living act is realized only in the act itself. This meeting is a spontaneous explosion of hopes. That is why it is a venture in prophetic poverty, supported and financed by no foundation, organized and publicized by no official group, but a living expression of the belief that there are now in our world new people, new poets who are not in tutelage to established political systems or cultural structures—whether communist or capitalist—but who dare to hope in their own vision of reality and of the future. This meeting is united in a flame of hope whose temperature has not yet been taken and whose effects have not yet been estimated, because it is a new fire. The reason for the fire cannot be apparent to one who is not warmed by it. The reason for being here will not be found until all have walked together, without afterthought, into contradictions and possibilities.

We believe that our future will be made by love and hope, not by violence or calculation. The Spirit of Life that has brought us together, whether in space or only in agreement, will make our encounter an epiphany of certainties we could not know in isolation.

The solidarity of poets is not planned and welded together with tactical convictions or matters of policy, since these are affairs of prejudice, cunning, and design. Whatever his failures, the poet is not a cunning man. His art depends on an ingrained innocence which he would lose in business, in politics, or in too organized a form of academic

life. The hope that rests on calculation has lost its innocence. We are banding together to defend our innocence.

(LE 371–72)

• • •

If we are to remain united against these falsehoods, against
all power that poisons man, and subjects him to the mystifications of bureaucracy, commerce, and the police state,
we must refuse the price tag.

For the poet there is precisely no magic. There is only
life in all its unpredictability and all its freedom. All magic
is a ruthless venture in manipulation, a vicious circle, a self-
fulfilling prophecy.

Word-magic is an impurity of language and of spirit in
which words, deliberately reduced to unintelligibility, appeal mindlessly to the vulnerable will. Let us deride and
parody this magic with other variants of the unintelligible,
if we want to. But it is better to prophesy than to deride. To
prophesy is not to predict, but to seize upon reality in its
moment of highest expectation and tension toward the
new. This tension is discovered not in hypnotic elation but
in the light of everyday existence. Poetry is innocent of pre-
diction because it is itself the fulfillment of all the momen-
tous predictions hidden in everyday life.

Poetry is the flowering of ordinary possibilities. It is the
fruit of ordinary and natural choice. This is its innocence
and dignity.

Let us not be like those who wish to make the tree bear
its fruit first and the flower afterward—a conjuring trick
and an advertisement. We are content if the flower comes
first and the fruit afterward, in due time. Such in the poetic
spirit.

(LE 372–73)

• • •

Let us obey life, and the Spirit of Life that calls us to be poets, and we shall harvest many new fruits for which the world hungers—fruits of hope that have never been seen before. With these fruits we shall calm the resentments and the rage of man.

Let us be proud that we are not witch doctors, only ordinary men.

Let us be proud that we are not experts in anything.

Let us be proud of the words that are given to us for nothing, not to teach anyone, not to confute anyone, not to prove anyone absurd, but to point beyond all objects into the silence where nothing can be said.

We are not persuaders. We are the children of the Unknown. We are the ministers of silence that is needed to cure all victims of absurdity who lie dying of a contrived joy. Let us then recognize ourselves for who we are: dervishes mad with secret therapeutic love which cannot be bought or sold, and which the politician fears more than violent revolution, for violence changes nothing. But love changes everything.

We are stronger than the bomb.

Let us then say "yes" to our own nobility by embracing the insecurity and abjection that a dervish existence entails.

In the *Republic* of Plato there was already no place for poets and musicians, still less for dervishes and monks. As for the technological Platos who think they now run the world we live in, they imagine they can tempt us with banalities and abstractions. But we can elude them merely by stepping into the Heraklitean river which is never crossed twice.

When the poet puts his foot in that ever-moving river,

poetry itself is born out of the flashing water. In that unique instant, the truth is manifest to all who are able to receive it.

No one can come near the river unless he walks on his own feet. He cannot come there carried in a vehicle.

No one can enter the river wearing the garments of public and collective ideas. He must feel the water on his skin. He must know that immediacy is for naked minds only, and for the innocent.

Come, dervishes: here is the water of life. Dance in it.

(LE 373–74)

• • •

The artist who expends all his efforts in convincing himself that he is not a non-artist or the anti-artist who struggles not to become "an artist" cannot justify his vexations by appealing to an ideal of freedom. What he needs is not an ideal of freedom, but at least a minimum of practical and subjective autonomy—freedom from the internalized emotional pressures by which society holds him down. I mean freedom of conscience. This is a spiritual value and its roots are ultimately religious. Hence my first principle is that since in our society everybody is already more or less concerned with a theoretical and doctrinaire approach to the question of art and freedom, maybe the artist himself has something better to do—namely his own job. There have grown up so many myths about the business of "being an artist" and living the special kind of life that artists are reputed to live, that if the artist is too concerned with "being an artist" he will never get around to doing any work. Hence it is to his advantage, first of all, to be free from myths about "Art" and even from myths about the threat which society offers to his "freedom." This applies, at least, to artists living in "the West," where in fact nobody is seriously interfering with his freedom. On the other hand, under Communism the poets and painters seem to be the most serious prophets of a genuine liberation for thought, life, and experience. They protest more articulately than anyone against the general servility to boredom and official stupidity.

Yet the artist who is held by dope or drink is just as much a prisoner of a corrupt commercial or political power structure as the artist who is held by the coercion of the Writer's Union. Each in his own way is turning out propaganda by producing something according to the dictates of the society in which he lives. The artist who is really free and chooses this particular servitude is perhaps less worthy of admiration than one who, being subject to all kinds of harassment, still makes the choice for which Sartre praised the men of the French resistance under Nazism.

(LE 376)

From "Louis Zukofsky—the Paradise Ear," 1966

ALL REALLY VALID POETRY (poetry that is fully alive and asserts its reality by its power to generate imaginative life) is a kind of recovery of paradise. Not that the poet comes up with a report that he, an unusual man, has found his own way back into Eden: but the living line and the generative association, the new sound, the music, the structure, are somehow grounded in a renewal of vision and hearing so that he who reads and understands recognizes that here is a new start, a new creation. Here the world gets another chance. Here man, here the reader discovers himself getting another start in life, in hope, in imagination, and why? Hard to say, but probably because the language itself is getting another chance, through the innocence, the teaching, the good faith, the honest senses of the workman poet.

(LE 128)

From a Letter to Ludovico Silva, April 27, 1967

Ludovico Silva was a Venezuelan poet (1937–1988) and the author of more than thirty books of poetry, essays, and literary criticism.

THE FUTURE OF POETRY: my reaction is totally positive. The poets have much to say and do: they have the same mission as the prophets in the technical world. They have to be the consciousness of the revolutionary man because they have the keys of the subconscious and of the great secrets of real life. But the governments are full of poet-killers and of anti-poets with machines to fabricate only death and nothing more. Then, the future of the poetry depends upon their freedom, the freedom of conscience and of creation. The future of poetry is also the future of the world. For one cannot truly believe in God if one does not believe in mankind as well: the poets will triumph. We will triumph. God is with the poets. That is why I am especially happy to know that *Boom* has some success with those who know how to read.

I send you some essays with my hug.

(CFT 230–31)

On Other Writers

Journal Entry, October 15, 1939

Proust and memory: to Proust experience seems to be valuable only after it has been transformed by memory. That is, he is not interested in the present: and I suppose while he was writing his other possible present experiences did not appeal to him: sick in bed. The "present time of things present" was unbearable. What kept attracting him was the "present time of things past." Actually what was important to him was writing—that is, writing was the one "present" he could put up with.

(RUN 57)

From a Letter to Mark Van Doren, January 28, 1941

Mark Van Doren (1894–1972) was a professor of English at Columbia College from 1920 to 1959. He was awarded the Pulitzer Prize for Poetry in 1939. Both Merton and Jack Kerouac took his Shakespeare class as under-graduates.

I WAS VERY SAD that Joyce died, and I hope he gets to heaven. His death was the same kind of news as that of the fall of Paris, to me.

(RTJ 10)

Journal Entry, August 14, 1948, Vigil of the Assumption

D YLAN THOMAS'S INTEGRITY as a poet makes me very ashamed of the verse I have been writing. We who say we love God: why are we not as anxious to be perfect in our art as we pretend we want to be in our service of God? If we do not try to be perfect in what we write, perhaps it is because we are not writing for God after all. In any case it is depressing that those who serve God and love Him sometimes write so badly, when those who do not believe in Him take pains to write so well. I am not talking about grammar and syntax, but about having something to say and saying it in sentences that are not half dead. Saint Paul and Saint Ignatius Martyr did not bother about grammar but they certainly knew how to write.

Imperfection is the penalty of rushing into print. And people who rush into print too often do so not because they really have anything to say, but because they think it is important for something by them to be in print. The fact that your subject may be very important in itself does not necessarily mean that what *you* have written about it is important. A bad book about the love of God remains a bad book, even though it may be about the love of God. There are many who think that because they have written about God, they have written good books. Then men pick up these books and say: if the ones who say they believe in God cannot find anything better than this to say about it, their religion cannot be worth much.

(SOJ 60–61)

Journal Entry, December 20, 1948, Vigil of Saint Thomas

RILKE'S NOTEBOOKS have so much power in them that they make me wonder why no one writes like that in monasteries. Not that there have not been better books written in monasteries, and books more serene. But monks do not seem to be able to write so well—and it is as if our professional spirituality sometimes veiled our contact with the naked realities inside us. It is a common failing of monks to lose themselves in a collective, professional personality—to let themselves be cast in a mold. Yet this mold does not seem to do away with what is useless or even unpleasant about some personalities. We cling to our eccentricities and our selfishness, but we do so in a way that is no longer interesting because it is after all mechanical and vulgar.

(SOJ 251)

Journal Entry, December 30, 1949

I LIKE KENNETH PATCHEN's *Dark Kingdom* but it does not do anything beyond interest the surface of my mind. It does not make a deep impression, and it cannot because it is only poetry. The only books [or writers] that move me deeply are the Bible, Saint John of the Cross, *The Cloud of Unknowing,* and a few others like that: Tauler, Saint Augustine, parts of Saint Bernard, Saint Gregory of Nyssa.

(SOJ 260)

From a Letter to Boris Pasternak, August 22, 1958

Boris Leonidovich Pasternak was born in Moscow in 1890 and died in 1960. Awarded the Nobel Prize for Literature in 1958, he was forced to decline the honor, expelled from the Soviet Writers' Union, and declared a traitor by the Soviet regime.

ALTHOUGH WE ARE SEPARATED by great distances and even greater barriers it gives me pleasure to speak to you as to one whom I feel to be a kindred mind. We are both poets—you a great one and I a very minor one. We share the same publisher in this country—New Directions. At least for our poetry; for your prose work is appearing under the Pantheon imprint and mine appears in another house.

I have not yet had the pleasure of reading your recent autobiography although I am familiar with the earlier one, *Safe Conduct,* by which I was profoundly impressed. It may surprise you when I say, in all sincerity, that I feel much more kinship with you, in your writing, than I do with most of the great modern writers in the West. That is to say that I feel that I can share your experience more deeply and with a greater intimacy and sureness, than that of writers like [James] Joyce whom I nevertheless so well like and understand. But when you write of your youth in the Urals, in Marburg, in Moscow, I feel as if it were my own experience, as if I were you.

With other writers I can share ideas, but you seem to communicate something deeper. It is as if we met on a deeper level of life on which individuals are not separate beings. In the language familiar to me as a Catholic monk, it is as if we were known to one another in God. This is a very simple and to me obvious expression for something quite normal and ordinary, and I feel no need to apologize for it. I am convinced that you understand me perfectly. It is true that a person always remains a person and utterly separate and apart from every other person. But it is equally true that each person is destined to reach with others an understanding and a unity which transcend individuality, and Russian tradition describes this with a concept we do not fully possess in the West—*sobornost.*

It gives me pleasure to send you under separate cover a kind of prose poem or meditation on Prometheus, which has been privately printed near here recently. At least you will like the handsome printing. I hope the book reaches you. I am writing to you in your village home near Moscow—of which I happened to read in an English magazine. If you get this letter, and not the book, I hope you will let me know. I will try again.

It is my intention to begin learning Russian in order to try to get into Russian literature in the original. It is very hard to get much in the way of translations. I would much prefer to read you in Russian, though it will probably be a long time before I am able to do so. What I have read of modern Russian poets in translation is to me very stimulating. I have no difficulty in admitting a certain lassitude and decadence in much Western literature. I like [Vladimir] Mayakovsky and also I am very much interested in [Velimir] Khlebnikov (is that how you spell it?). What do you think of him? [Aleksandr] Blok of course I find very interesting. What about the new poets? Are there some good ones? Whom do you recommend? Do you know of the many very fine poets there have been in Latin America? I am particularly fond of a great Negro poet of Brazil, Jorge de Lima. [Pablo] Neruda, of Chile, is probably well known in the USSR and I presume you know him.

My dear Pasternak, it is a joy to write to you and to thank you for your fine poetry and your great prose. A voice like yours is of great importance for all mankind in our day—so too is a voice like that of [Dmitry] Shosta-kovich. The Russian leaders do not perhaps realize to the full how important and how great you are for Russia and for the world. Whatever may lie ahead for the world, I be-lieve that men like yourself and I hope myself also may have the chance to enter upon a dialogue that will really lead to peace and to a fruitful age for man and his world. Such peace and fruitfulness are spiritual realities to which you already have access, though others do not.

(CFT 87–88)

From a Letter to Czeslaw Milosz, December 6, 1958

Milosz was born in Seteiniai, Lithuania, in 1911 and died in 2004. He won the Nobel Prize for Literature in 1980.

HAVING READ YOUR REMARKABLE BOOK *The Captive Mind* I find it necessary to write to you, as without your help I am unable to pursue certain lines of thought which this book suggests. I would like to ask you a couple of questions and hope you will forgive this intrusion.

First of all I would like to say that I found your book to be one of the most intelligent and stimulating it has been my good fortune to read for a very long time. It is an im-portant book, which makes most other books on the pres-ent state of man look abjectly foolish. I find it especially important for myself in my position as a monk, a priest, and a writer. It is obvious that a Catholic writer in such a time as ours has an absolute duty to confine himself to reality and not waste his time in verbiage and empty rationalizations. Unfortunately, as I have no need to point out to you, most of us do this and much worse. The lamentable, pitiable emptiness of so much Catholic writing, including much of my own, is only too evident. Your book has come to me, then, as something I can call frankly "spiritual," that is to say, as the inspiration of much thought, meditation, and prayer about my own obligations to the rest of the human race, and about the predicament of us all.

It seems to me that, as you point out, and as other writers like yourself say or imply (Koestler, Camus etc.), there *has to be* a third position, a position of integrity, which refuses subjection to the pressures of the two massive groups ranged against each other in the world. It is quite simply obvious that the future, in plain dialectical terms, rests with those of us who risk our heads and our necks and everything in the difficult, fantastic job of finding out the new position, the ever-changing and moving "line" that is NO line at all because it cannot be traced out by political dogmatists. And that is the difficulty, and the challenge. I am the last in the world to pretend to know anything about it. One thing I do know, is that anyone who is interested in God Who is Truth, has to break out of the ready-made shells of the "captive" positions that offer their convenient escapes from freedom—one who loves freedom must go through the painful experience of seeking it, perhaps without success. And for my part, this letter represents a hearty peck at the inside of my own particular kind of shell, the nature and hardness of which I leave you to imagine.

(CFT 54–55)

From a Letter to Boris Pasternak,
October 23, 1958

W HAT A GREAT JOY it was to receive your two letters. It has given me much food for thought, this bare fact of the communication between us: at a time when our two countries are unable to communicate with one another seriously and sincerely, but spend millions communicating with the moon. . . . No, the great business of our time is this: for one man to find himself in another one who is on the other side of the world. Only by such contacts can there be peace, can the sacredness of life be preserved and developed and the image of God manifest itself in the world.

Since my first letter to you I have obtained and read the book [*Doctor Zhivago*] published by Pantheon, and it has been a great and rewarding experience. First of all it has astounded me with the great number of sentences that I myself might have written, and in fact perhaps have written. Just one example at random: I am bringing out a book on sacred art in which one of the theses is practically this: "All genuine art resembles and continues the Revelation of St. John." This is to me so plain and so obvious that as a result I have seriously questioned the claim of the Renaissance to have produced much genuinely religious art. . . . But enough of the small details.

The book is a world in itself, a sophiological world, a paradise and a hell, in which the great mystical figures of Yurii and Lara stand out as Adam and Eve and though they walk in darkness walk with their hand in the hand of God. The earth they walk upon is sacred because of them. It is the sacred earth of Russia, with its magnificent destiny which remains hidden for it in the plans of God. To me the most overwhelmingly beautiful and moving passage is the short, tranquil section in the Siberian town where Yurii lying in the other room listens through the open door to the religious conversation of Lara and the other woman. This section is as it were the "eye" of a hurricane—that calm center of whirlwind, the emptiness in which is truth, spoken in all its fullness, in quiet voice, by lamplight. But it is hard to pick out any one passage. All through the book great waves of beauty break over the reader like waves of a newly discovered sea. Through you I have gained a great wondering love for the Urals (here I cannot accept your repudiation of the earlier books, where I first discovered this). The train journey to the east is magnificent. The exciting and rich part about the partisans is very interesting. Of course, I find in the book too little of Uncle Nikolai and his ideas—this is my only complaint and perhaps it is unjust, for his ideas speak in everything that happens.

Am I right in surmising that the ideas in this book run closely parallel to those in [Vladimir] Soloviev's *Meaning of Love?* There is a great similarity. Both works remind us to fight our way out of complacency and realize that all our work remains yet to be done, the work of transformation which is the work of love, and love alone. I need not tell you that I also am one who has tried to learn deeply from Dostoevsky's Grand Inquisitor, and I am passionately convinced that this is the most important of all lessons for our time. It is important here, and there. Equally important everywhere.

Shall I perhaps tell you how I know Lara, where I have met her? It is a simple enough story but obviously I do not tell it to people—you are the fourth who knows it, and there seems to be no point in a false discreetness that might restrain me from telling you since it is clear that we have so much in common.

One night I dreamt that I was sitting with a very young Jewish girl of fourteen or fifteen, and that she suddenly manifested a very deep and pure affection for me and embraced me so that I was moved to the depths of my soul. I learned that her name was "Proverb," which I thought very simple and beautiful. And also I thought: "She is of the race of Saint Anne." I spoke to her of her name, and she did not seem to be proud of it, because it seemed that the other young girls mocked her for it. But I told her that it was a very beautiful name, and there the dream ended. A few days later when I happened to be in a nearby city [Louisville], which is very rare for us, I was walking alone in the crowded street and suddenly saw that everybody was Proverb and that in all of them shone her extraordinary beauty and purity and shyness, even though they did not know who they were and were perhaps ashamed of their names—because they were mocked on account of them. And they did not know their real identity as the Child so dear to God who, from before the beginning, was playing in His sight all days, playing in the world.

Thus you are initiated into the scandalous secret of a monk who is in love with a girl, and a Jew at that! One cannot expect much from monks these days. The heroic asceticism of the past is no more.

(CFT 89–91)

From "The Pasternak Affair," 1959

PASTERNAK STANDS FIRST OF ALL for the great spiritual values that are under attack in our materialistic world. He stands for the freedom and nobility of the individual person, for man the image of God, for man in whom God dwells. For Pasternak, the person is and must always remain prior to the collectivity. He stands for courageous, independent loyalty to his own conscience, and for the refusal to compromise with slogans and rationalizations imposed by compulsion. Pasternak is fighting for man's true freedom, his true creativity, against the false and empty humanism of the Marxists—for whom man does not yet truly exist. Over against the technological jargon and the empty scientism of modern man, Pasternak sets creative symbolism, the power of imagination and of intuition, the glory of liturgy, and the fire of contemplation. But he does so in new words, in a new way. He speaks for all that is sanest and most permanently vital in religious and cultural tradition, but with the voice of a man of our own time.

(LE 56)

• • •

Like Dostoevsky, Pasternak holds that man's future depends on his ability to work his way out from under a continuous succession of authoritarian rulers who promise him happiness at the cost of his freedom. Like Dostoevsky, also, Pasternak insists that the fruit of Christ's Incarnation, Death, and Resurrection, is that true freedom has at least become possible: but that man, ignoring the real meaning of the New Testament, prefers to evade the responsibility of his vocation and continues to live "under the law." This is not a new complaint: it goes back to St. Paul.

Ironically enough, one of the most brilliant analyses of man's alienation came from the pen of Marx. Modern Russia, while paying lip service to Marx's theory on this point, has forgotten his full meaning. Yet in so doing, the Soviets have brought out the inner contradiction of Marx's thought: for the complete spiritual alienation of man which Marx ascribed in part to religion has been brought about by militant atheism, as well as by the economic system which claims to be built on an orthodox Marxian foundation. It is of course not fair to blame Stalin's police state directly on Marx, though Marx cannot be absolved from indirect responsibility.

(LE 71)

• • •

All great writing is in some sense revolutionary. Life itself is revolutionary, because it constantly strives to surpass itself. And if history is to be something more than the record of society's bogging down in meaningless formalities to justify the crimes of men, then a book that is at the same time great in its own right, and moreover lands with a tremendous impact on the world of its time, deserves an important place in history. The reason why *Dr. Zhivago* is significant is precisely that it stands so far above politics. This, among other things, places it in an entirely different category from Dudintsev's *Not by Bread Alone*. Attempts to involve Pasternak in the Cold War have been remarkable above all by their futility. The cloud of misunderstandings and accusations that surrounded the affair did not engulf Pasternak: the confusion served principally to emphasize the distance which separated him from his accusers and his admirers alike.

(LE 41–42)

• • •

Both as a writer and as a man, Pasternak stands out as a sign of contradiction in our age of materialism, collectivism, and power politics. His spiritual genius is essentially and powerfully solitary. Yet his significance does not lie precisely in this. Rather it lies in the fact that his very solitude made him capable of extraordinarily intimate and understanding contacts with men all over the face of the earth. The thing that attracted people to Pasternak was not a social or political theory, it was not a formula for the unification of mankind, not a collectivist panacea for all the evils in the world: it was the man himself, the truth that was in him, his simplicity, his direct contact with life, and the fact that he was full of the only revolutionary force that is capable of producing anything new: he is full of love.

(LE 42)

• • •

Language is not merely the material or the instrument which the poet uses. This is the sin of the Soviet ideologist for whom language is simply a mine of terms and formulas which can be pragmatically exploited. When in the moment of inspiration the poet's creative intelligence is married with the inborn wisdom of human language (the Word of God and Human Nature—Divinity and Sophia) then in the very flow of new and individual intuitions, the poet utters the voice of that wonderful and mysterious world of God-manhood—it is the transfigured, spiritualized, and divinized cosmos that speaks through him, and through him utters its praise of the Creator.

(LE 49)

• • •

Language, the home and receptacle of beauty and meaning, itself begins to think and speak for man and turns wholly into music, not in terms of sonority but in terms of the impetuousness and power of its inward flow. Then, like the current of a mighty river polishing stones and turning wheels by its very movement, the flow of speech creates in passing, by virtue of its own laws, meter and rhythm and countless other relationships, which are even more important, but which are as yet unexplored, insufficiently recognized, and unnamed. At such moments, Yurii Andreievitch felt that the main part of the work was being done not by him but by a superior power that was above him and directed him, namely the movement of universal thought and poetry in its present historical stage and in the one to come. And he felt himself to be only the occasion, the fulcrum, needed to make this movement possible.

(LE 49)

• • •

The great success of *Dr. Zhivago* is by no means attributable to the mere fact that it happens to contain sentences which level devastating blows against the Communist mentality. Anyone with any perception can see that these blows fall, with equal power, on every form of materialistic society. They fall upon most of the gross, pervasive, and accepted structures of thought and life which go to make up our changing world. The book is successful not because these blows are dealt, but because, as they land, we gradually begin to realize that Pasternak seems to know what is wrong. He seems to know what has happened to our spiritual freedom. He seems to realize why it is that most of the world's talk about freedom, peace, happiness, hope for the future is just talk and nothing more. He knows all too well that such talk is only a palliative for despair. But at the same time he has a true and solid hope to offer.

(LE 67)

• • •

Pasternak has become a best seller and a widely read author in the West, but he will always be a writer's writer. His greatest impact has been on the *writers* of the West. He has received letters from all kinds of people, but especially from other writers, in many different countries, not the least being Camus and Mauriac. Pasternak answered all these letters with profound warmth of understanding, and those who were privileged to be in contact with him felt that he had given them much more than they expected— an inspiration and sense of direction which they had ceased to hope for from any other writer!

We have learned from Pasternak that we must never yield to the great temptation offered by Communism to the writer. I do not mean the temptation to be a member of a privileged and respected class, but the far more insidious one of becoming a "writer for the future." Surely there is something apocalyptic about the sinister complacency with which Communism, which has hitherto proved effective only in killing writers or ruining them, proposes itself as Master of the future of literature. "Write for us, you will be remembered forever in the Kingdom of the Messiah who has now come! Refuse our offer, and you will be buried with the world that we are about to bury."

(LE 78–79)

From a Letter to Sister Therese Lentfoehr, SDS, January 18, 1960

HAVE YOU READ THE POEMS of Brother Antoninus [William Everson]? Very very fine. I am most happy with their rugged, austere, monastic quality. Serious and deeply sincere, with a wonderful sense of the ambivalence of life and the reality of sin and of God's mercy. That is the very stuff our life is made of, and modern Catholic devotion tries to escape it with sentiment. There is no escape. It has to be faced squarely. He does this, and I am grateful. I went over some of his poems with the novices over the holidays.

(RTJ 235)

From a Letter to Henry Miller, July 9, 1962

Henry Miller (1891–1980), American author of The Tropic of Cancer, *lived in France during the 1930s before taking up residence in Big Sur, California, in 1942.*

I T WAS GOOD TO HEAR FROM YOU. I have often thought of writing to you, and usually that is the first thing that comes into my mind when I am reading something of yours, like the earlier part of *Big Sur* [*and the Oranges of Hieronymus Bosch*] for example, or parts of the *Colossus of Maroussi* (which I think is a tremendous and important book). I have always refrained because it is foolish for me to write letters anyway, and then I know you have little time. I am sure you must get much the same kind of mail that I do, including the poets who send you their collected works in weekly installments, and the anonymous painter who, today, sent me a large abstraction. This is all fine, but where does one get the time to collect his thoughts and come up with some kind of an intelligent word, in the presence of so many manifestations? I detest writing letters about which I do not think, at least when thought is called for. It is perhaps fortunate that there are some letters one can write without thinking: business letters.

They come out like sweat.

One of the things I have wanted to discuss with you is

our common admiration for [Jean] Giono.[4] Something must be done to get a good selection of his stuff published in English—unless perhaps such a thing already exists, without my knowing of it. Recently I managed to get hold of some of his shorter prose pieces about Provence, and they are remarkable. His view of things is the sane one, the one that must be preserved as a basis for some kind of vestigial humanism, if humanism is to remain possible. I have not read his historical novels, and there are lots of his novels about Provence that I have never come across: as I say, I have read mostly essays. I think New Directions ought to do something with him.

I expect to find a lot of the same in the [Joseph] Delteil[5] book which arrived the other day. I have not got very far into it yet, but I think something ought to be done with it in this country, nor is there much difficulty in that.

Does Delteil read English? He might like the banned book I have just written (you are not the only one, you see!) about peace [*Peace in the Post-Christian Era*]. My book is not satisfactory however, because I was fool enough to try to write one that the censors would approve, and this led to compromise and stupidity. And in the end they did not approve anyway. Does he, do you, know of Fr. Hervé Chaigne, the Franciscan who is a Gandhian and involved in the non-violent movement in France?

Returning to Giono: I am thinking a lot of Provence because I am doing some work on the early monastic liter-

4. French novelist (1895–1950), wrote about Provençal life, nature, pacifism. Author of *The Man Who Planted Trees*.—Ed.
5. Nonconformist French writer (1894–1978), left Paris for southern France to live the life of the peasant/writer. Not widely translated—known in the United States for the 1928 film *The Passion of Joan of Arc*, based upon one of his books.—Ed.

ature surrounding the Provençal monasteries of the 5th century, particularly Lérins. It was a great movement. That and Cassiodorus[6] too, in Italy. One thing I envy you is your freedom to get around to such places.

I have not seen your latest books, but I just asked J. Laughlin to send me a couple. Have you seen *New Seeds of Contemplation?* He probably sent you that. I am sending along the banned book with a couple of other items that we put out here with a mimeograph machine, run by a monk with an eyeshade who lives in a room full of birds.

This much for now. Do keep in touch with me, especially about Giono, and I will write some more about Delteil later. And keep speaking out. You are in my prayers.

(CFT 274–75)

From a Letter to Henry Miller, *August 7, 1962*

I AM IN THE MIDDLE OF *The Wisdom of the Heart* and it is you at your best. There is very fine material everywhere, one insight on top of another. The opening piece starting from Lawrence is full of arresting thought, most important for a writer to read. When you write as you do in the thing on Benno you are at your very best, this is marvelous. As I say I am going along with you all the way with *The Wisdom of the Heart.* They sent me also the *Colossus* which I already had but had lent to someone, and lent books never come back. And *The Time of the Assassins,* which is going to mean much.

The English Carmelites sent me their review about

6. Roman Senator (490–585) who became a monk and left behind a substantial and varied body of writing. Founded two monasteries.—Ed.

those two late-nineteenth-century people, but I thought all they had to say was very good indeed. How would it be if I sent them a poem? What do you think?

Scotland drove me nuts when I was there in childhood, but I have all kinds of dreams about getting on one of those outlying islands. Maybe this is the worst delusion. I wonder what you will think of it. The people as I remember them were absurd, and especially the place used to be full of Englishmen who wouldn't call a brook anything but a burn, and who stuffed their stupid faces with scones at all hours of the day and night while a character walked up and down playing the bagpipes to them. They deserved it.

I bet you are totally right about Ireland. The combination of faith and poverty has now become one of the things that cries out to heaven for vengeance, loud enough for the vengeance to be quite near.

In the whole question of religion today: all I can say is I wish I could really see what is there to see. Nobody can see the full dimension of the problem, which is more than a problem, it is one of those things you read about in the Apocalypse. There are no problems in the Apocalypse, just monsters. This one is a monster.

The religion of religious people tends at times to poke out a monster head just when you are beginning to calm down and get reassured. The religion of half-religious people doesn't tend: it bristles with heads. The horns, the horns with eyes on the end of them, the teeth, the teeth with eyes in them, the eyes as sharp as horns, the dull eyes, the ears that now listen to all the stars and decode their message into something about business upswing.

This is the greatest orgy of idolatry the world has ever known, and it is not generally thought by believers that idolatry is the greatest and fundamental sin. It is absolutely not thought, it is not credited, it cannot be accepted, and if you go around and speak of idolatry they will fall down and laugh and the heads of the monsters will roll and wag like the biggest carnival you ever saw. But precisely the greatest and most absurd difficulty of our time is keeping disentangled from the idols, because you cannot touch anything that isn't defiled with it: anything you buy, anything you sell, anything you give even. And of course the significance of it is absolutely lost. Anyone who sells out to even a small, inoffensive, bargain-cheap idol has alienated himself and put himself into the statue and has to act like it, which is he has to be dead.

The religion of non-religious people tends to be clear of religious idols and is in many ways much less pseudo. But on the other hand, they often have no defense against the totalitarian kind, which end up being bigger and worse.

I frankly don't have an answer. As a priest I ought, of course, to be able to give Christ's answer. But unfortunately . . . it is no longer a matter of answers. It is a time perhaps of great spiritual silence.

I must really read Emerson, I never have. Except little bits that I have liked a lot. Thoreau of course I admire tremendously. He is one of the only reasons why I felt justified in becoming an American citizen. He and Emily Dickinson, and some of my friends, and people like yourself. It is to me a great thing that you say I am like the transcendentalists. I will try to be worthy of that. This is not just something we can elect to try as a boy scout project: it is a serious duty for all of us, and woe to us if we do not take it for what it is.

The time is short, and all the idols are moving. They are so full of people that they are becoming at last apparently animated and when they get fully into action the result will be awful. It will be like the clashing of all the planets. Strange that the individual is the only power that is left. And though his power is zero, zero has great power when one understands it and knows where to place it.

(CFT 274–78)

From a Letter to Donald Fiene, November 22, 1962

I WAS INTERESTED IN YOUR LETTER about your work on [J. D.] Salinger, and I will try to give you some sort of an answer to your inquiry. I am afraid it is not going to amount to much, however, and I suppose the reason is that I am almost the perfectly wrong person to answer a question and give an opinion on Salinger.

First of all, what it amounts to mostly is that I have nothing whatever against him. And secondly I have not really read him. Why should I have anything against a man I have not really read? I am not the sort of person that opens a book and sees a few four letter words and immediately throws it in the wastebasket after purifying the whole place with some kind of deodorant.

What have I read of his? I started *Franny and Zooey.* That is to say, I started Franny, and after that I started Zooey. I thought it was well written. I thought the people were alive, and I could see where one would get deeply absorbed in their concerns, but let me put it this way: I am profoundly engrossed in the 12th century school of Chartres, and in Zen (which I understand comes later in Zooey?) and in Sufism, and in some novices I am supposed to be teaching about the monastic life, and in the peace movement, and in poetry of a sort. My reaction to *Franny and Zooey* was simply that it was keeping me from something else in which I was really interested. I have absolutely nothing against *Franny* or *Zooey*. I am glad they had people who wrote such nice letters to them. But this is what I walked away from twenty years ago and it is just very remote, it doesn't come through anymore. I am sorry, this may be a confession that I have drifted away from the human race, though I don't think even Salinger would interpret it that way.

On the other hand one of the young priests in the monastery was floating on a cloud after reading *Franny and Zooey,* and as a matter of fact he was the one who lent me the book. I can see where he perhaps needed the kind of stimulation the book would give, a reminder of what people feel and say to each other and the tangles they get in, because perhaps he did not get a big enough bite of all that before he came in here. I had plenty of big bites of it, I stuffed myself with it, and now I am through. It is like last year's breakfast. And this, I conclude, is a purely subjective judgment which really has no value at all for the purposes of a work like yours. But if you want to quote it for any reason, by all means go ahead.

Let me add this: when I was outside, twenty-two or -three years ago, I used to like Saroyan and I had a girl-friend who was in one of his plays, etc. Then this was all very important to me. You see what I mean? I have had it all before. My train has gone way past the station. I am old, well, middle-aged. But let me encourage you with your book and with your writing, because it sounds right for you, and this is what you should do.

(RTJ 324–25)

From a Letter to Napoleón Chow,
May 14, 1963

T HE PROTEST OF THE BEATNIKS, while having a certain element of sincerity, is largely a delusion. It is a
false revolution, sterile and impotent, and its few flashes of
originality, its attempts to express compassion, only increase the delusion. I am afraid the beats are to a great extent infantile. Yet this much can be said for them: their very
formlessness may perhaps be something that is in their
favor. It may perhaps enable them to reject most of the false
solutions and deride the "square" propositions of the deca-
dent liberalism around them. It may perhaps prepare them
to go in the right direction.

(CFT 170)

From a Letter to M. R. Chandler,
July 19, 1963

M. R. Chandler of the San Francisco Examiner *invited
Merton to respond to a questionnaire.*

I HOPE THESE ANSWERS are satisfactory. I read a lot in
Latin, French, and Spanish, besides English, and I always have at least three books going at the same time. I
tried to keep it simple and understandable, and hope I have
not failed.

One question you have not asked: about authors whom
one might consider too little known and too little read. One
of these in my opinion would be the late Ananda K.
Coomaraswamy, whose field was Oriental art, but who actually had a great deal to say about the meeting of Eastern

and Western culture. This is a topic of vital importance today. One rarely sees this great man in paperbacks, though almost everyone manages to get there at some time or other.

Reading, to my mind, means reading *books*. I don't think magazines alone meet the requirements, because even with a heavy magazine you can get in the habit of skipping around (of course you can do this in a book too). But normally with a book you have to get down to business and keep on reading continuously, so that with a book with any substance at all you are forced to think. The real joy of reading is not in the reading itself but in the thinking which it stimulates and which may go beyond what is said in the book.

Traditionally, for a monk, reading is inseparable from *meditation*. I would be interested in seeing the column in which you make use of this material.

[The following are the questions, with Merton's answers:]

1. *Name the last three books you have read.*

The Platform Scripture of Hui Neng, translated by Wing Tsit Chan
The Proslogion by St. Anselm of Canterbury
A Different Drummer by William Melvin Kelley

2. *Name the books you are reading now.*

Homo Ludens: A Study of the Play Element in Culture by John Huizinga
Ratio Verae Theologiae (*The Real Meaning of Theology*) by Erasmus
The Historian and Character by David Knowles

3. *Books you intend to read.*

Apology to the Iroquois by Edmund Wilson
The Silent Rebellion: Anglican Religious Communities, 1845–1900 by A. M. Allchin
Cur Deus Homo by St. Anselm of Canterbury

4. *Books that have influenced you.*

Poetic Works of William Blake
Plays of Aeschylus and Sophocles
Summa Theologica of St. Thomas Aquinas
Sermons of Meister Eckhart
De Doctrina Christiana, Confessions, and *Sermons on Psalms*
   of St. Augustine
Rule of St. Benedict
The Bhagavad-Gita
The Imitation of Christ, etc.

5. *Why have these books been an influence on you?*

These books and others like them have helped me to discover the real meaning of my life, and have made it possible for me to get out of the confusion and meaninglessness of an existence completely immersed in the needs and passivities fostered by a culture in which sales are everything.

6. *Name a book everyone should read.*

Besides the Bible (taken for granted and not included above) and such classics as *The Imitation of Christ,* I would select a *contemporary book* which I consider to be of vital importance and which I think everyone should read at this time: *The Fire Next Time* by James Baldwin.

7. *Why this book?*

This is the most forceful statement about a crisis that is of immediate importance to every American, and indirectly affects the whole world today. It is something that people have to know about. The Negro has been trying to make himself heard: in this book he succeeds.

(WTF 165–66)

From a Letter to James Baldwin, No Date, 1963

James Baldwin (1924–1987), a novelist and essayist born and raised in Harlem, is the author of The Fire Next Time *(1963), the book that moved Merton to write to him.*

Y OU CANNOT EXPECT to write as you do without getting letters like this. One has to write, and I am sure you have received lots of letters already that say better than I can what this will try to say.

First of all, you are right all down the line. You exaggerate nowhere. You know exactly what you are talking about, and as a matter of fact it is really news to nobody (that is precisely one of your points). I have said the same myself, much more mildly and briefly, and far less well, in print so it is small wonder that I agree with you.

But the point is that this is one of the great realities of our time. For Americans it is perhaps the crucial truth, and all the other critical questions that face us are involved in this one.

It is certainly a matter for joy that you have at least said so much, and in the place where you have said it. It will be read and understood. But as I went through column after column [in the *New Yorker*] I was struck, as I am sure you were, by the ads all along each side of your text. What a commentary! They prove you more right than you could have imagined.

They go far beyond anything you have said. What force they lend to all your statements. No one could have dreamed up more damning evidence to illustrate what you say.

Sometimes I am convinced that there cannot be a way out of this. Humanly there is no hope, at least on the white side (that is where I unfortunately am). I don't see any courage or any capacity to grasp even the smallest bit of the enormous truth about ourselves. Note, I speak as a Catholic priest. We still see the whole thing as a sort of abstract exercise in ethics, when we see it at all. We don't see we are killing our own hope and the hope of the world.

You are very careful to make explicit the non-Christian attitude you take, and I respect this because I understand that this is necessary for you and I do not say this as an act of tolerant indulgence. It is in some sense necessary for me, too, because I am only worth so much as a priest, as I am able to see what the non-Christian sees. I am in most things right with you and the only point on which I disagree is that I think your view is fundamentally religious, genuinely religious, and therefore has to be against conventional religiosity. If you do not agree, it does not matter very much.

The other day I was talking to an African priest from Ghana. The impression I always get in talking to Africans is that they have about ten times as much reality as we have. This of course is not an accurate way of speaking: I think what it really expresses, this "sense," is the awareness of complementarity, the awareness of a reality in him which completes some lack in myself, and not of course an intuition of an absolute ontological value of a special essence. And I think as you yourself have suggested, that this is the whole story: there is not one of us, individually, racially, socially, who is fully complete in the sense of having in himself *all* the excellence of all humanity. And that this excellence, this totality, is built up out of the contributions of the particular parts of it that we all can share with one another. I am therefore not completely human until I have found myself in my African and Asian and Indonesian brother because he has the part of humanity which I lack.

The trouble is that we are supposed to be, and in a way we are, complete in ourselves. And we cherish the illusion that this completeness is not just a potential, but that it is finally realized from the very start, and that the notion of having to find something of ourselves only after a long search and after the gift of ourselves to others, does not apply to us. This illusion, which makes the white man imagine he does not need the Negro, enables him to think he can treat the Negro as an "object" and do what he likes with him. Indeed, in order to prove that his illusion is true, he goes ahead and treats the Negro in the way we know. He has to.

At the heart of the matter then is man's contempt for truth, and the substitution of his "self" for reality. His image is his truth. He believes in his specter and sacrifices human beings to his specter. This is what we are doing, and this is not Christianity or any other genuine religion: it is barbarity.

We cannot afford to have contempt for any truth, but least of all for a truth as urgent in our lives as this one. Hence, I want to give you all the moral support I can, which isn't much. I know you are more than fatigued with well-meaning white people clapping you on the shoulder and saying with utmost earnestness, "We are right with you," when of course we are right with ourselves and not in any of the predicaments you are in at all. What I will say is that I am glad I am not a Negro because I probably would never be able to take it: but that I recognize in conscience that I have a duty to try to make my fellow whites stop doing the things they do and see the problem in a different light. This does not presuppose an immediate program, or a surge of optimism, because I am still convinced that there is almost nothing to be done that will have any deep effect or make any real difference.

I am not in a position to be completely well informed on this issue, anyway. If you think of anything I ought to know about, I would be grateful if you put it in an envelope and send it down. I hope your article will have done some good. The mere fact that truth has been told is already a very great good in itself.

(CFT 244–46)

From a Letter to Walker Percy, January 1964

The novelist Walker Percy (1916–1990) studied medicine at Columbia University. The Moviegoer *won the National Book Award in 1961.*

THERE IS NO EASY WAY to thank you for your book. Not only are the good words about books all used up and ruined, but the honesty of *The Moviegoer* makes one more sensitive than usual about the usual nonsense. With reticence and malaise, then, I think your book is right on the target.

For a while I was going around saying it was too bad guys like Hemingway were dead, as if I really thought it.

You are right all the time, not just sometimes. You are

right all the time. You know just when to change and look at something else. Never too much of anyone. Just enough of Sharon. The reason the book is true is that you always stop at the point where more talk would have been false, untrue, confusing, irrelevant. It is not that what you say is true. It is neither true nor false, it points in the right direction, where there is something that has not been said and you know enough not to try to say it.

Hence you are one of the most hopeful existentialists I know of. I suppose it was inevitable that an American existentialist should have a merry kind of nausea after all, and no one reproaches you for this or anything else. It is truer than the viscous kind.

I think you started with the idea that Bolling would be a dope but he refused to be, and that is one of the best things about the book. Nice creative ambiguities in which the author and the character dialogue silently and wrestle for a kind of autonomy.

As for Southern aunts, if they are like that you can keep them. (But I praise the Southern aunt's last speech too. Insufferable, the last gasp.)

All this says nothing about how I was stirred up by the book. It should be read by the monks for a first lesson in humility. But I guess they would be bowled over by Sharon, so I better not hand it around to the novices.

(CFT 281–82)

From "Flannery O'Connor—a Prose Elegy," 1964

THE KEY WORD to Flannery's stories probably is "respect." She never gave up examining its ambiguities and its decay. In this bitter dialectic of half-truths that have become endemic to our system, she probed our very life— its conflicts, its falsities, its obsessions, its vanities. Have we become an enormous complex organization of spurious reverences? Respect is continually advertised, and we are still convinced that we respect "everything good"—when we know too well that we have lost the most elementary respect even for ourselves. Flannery saw this and saw, better than others, what it implied.

She wrote in and out of the anatomy of a word that became genteel, then self-conscious, then obsessive, finally dying of contempt, but kept calling itself "respect." Contempt for the child, for the stranger, for the woman, for the Negro, for the animal, for the white man, for the farmer, for the country, for the preacher, for the city, for the world, for reality itself. Contempt, contempt, so that in the end the gestures of respect they kept making to themselves and to each other and to God became desperately obscene.

(LE 159)

From a Letter to Edward Gerdes, April 18, 1964

THE BOOK YOU REFER TO is by Ayn Rand, right? I have not read it, but I tried another of hers and was bored to death. Couldn't make it at all. The philosophy is moronic.

The best critique of her thought I have seen is in a magazine called *New University Thought* published in Chicago. I don't have the address. For books that would provide principles which would correct her view, anything by Jacques Maritain, especially on morals.

From my point of view her philosophy is an organized egoism which is based on a completely illusory idea of the "self" and of the "person." This woman just does not know who she is. She strikes me as sick, alienated, and trying to cover up with a lot of brave noise. However the chief argument against following her principles is life itself. Anyone who lives according to her program will soon find out how well it works. Unfortunately there are too many people trying it all the time.

(RTJ 331–32)

From a Letter to Mr. L. Dickson, September 12, 1965

Mr. Dickson managed a bookstore at the University of Delaware in Newark.

I WILL BE GLAD to say something about the importance of *reading* in college since I know, from my own personal experience as an undergraduate and then a graduate student at Columbia, that reading and personal contacts in college can be absolutely decisive in a person's life.

It seems to me that a man or a woman goes to college not just to get a degree and a good job, but first of all to find himself and establish his true identity. You cannot go through life as a mask or as a well-functioning biological machine. Man is a being whose reality cannot be left entirely to forces outside himself, nature, society, events. We become real in proportion as we accept the real possibilities that are presented to us, and *choose from them freely and realistically* for ourselves. This act of choice implies a capacity to judge, therefore to think. It implies some kind of personal philosophy and a personal faith.

The reason why judgment and decisions are so important today is that a person, especially in college, is suddenly presented with such an overwhelming amount of material—ideologies, philosophies and pseudo-philosophies, religions and religious fads, movements in art, literature, politics, and new developments in science and technology—that he *has* to make a choice somewhere. If he fails to choose, he is lost in a confusion of contradictory notions that end up by meaning absolutely nothing. In which case he can either go crazy, or else become an insufferable square with a few mechanically pronounced dogmas instead of genuine thought.

Therefore, if a man is going to make authentic judgments and do some thinking for himself, he is going to have to renounce the passivity of a subject that merely sits and "takes in" what is told him, whether in class, or in front of the TV, or in the other mass media. This means serious and independent reading, and it also means articulate discussion.

If this letter will encourage students to read more widely, more critically, more eagerly, and if it helps someone to find books that will revolutionize his life, then I am glad to have written it. I might mention, though, that the quality of the books one reads and of the thoughts one "buys" certainly does make a difference. The mere fact that an idea is new and exciting does not necessarily make it true. Truth is important and the whole purpose of thinking is to be able to tell the difference between what is true and what only looks good.

I don't care whether or not the readers of this letter buy *my* books. But I might mention a few authors who have helped me a lot. Among moderns: Maritain, Gilson, Karl Barth, Camus, Pieper, Pasternak, Fromm, Eliot, Jaspers, Gandhi, Guardini, Suzuki. Among writers of the past: Plato, Lao Tzu, Confucius, Plotinus, St. Augustine, St. Thomas, St. Anselm, St. John of the Cross, Dante, Shakespeare, Cervantes, Pascal, Blake, Kierkegaard, and of course above all the Bible.

(WTF 168–69)

A Letter to Harry J. Cargas,
February 14, 1966

The late Harry James Cargas was professor of literature and language at Webster University and author of thirty-two books.

OKAY, A WORD ABOUT Thoreau since you ask.
The only references to him in my writing are few and I think really only one in *The Sign of Jonas*. And I do not know exactly where. I don't think I have any unpublished references to him either. I do remember once saying to Mark Van Doren in a letter (unpublished, I think. I don't believe it is in the letter section of *Seeds of Destruction*) that Thoreau and Emily Dickinson made me glad of being an American.

At Columbia I had Joseph Wood Krutch as one of my English professors, as well as Mark Van Doren. Both Thoreau men, but I did not have them in any class where Thoreau was treated. I liked Krutch and we got along very well (he gave me all A's and in fact an A+ on some of the work I did for him). Hence it is not so much that I was indoctrinated with Thoreau's ideas as that I have always agreed with his outlook and with those who see things the same way. In fact I did not seriously read him until I came to the monastery, and the one book of his that I have really read is *Walden*. I am living a Walden-like sort of life now, as a matter of fact. Some of my students have acquired a great liking for him here in the monastery. In fact, however, I have been attacked by a rather stuffy old professor in Rome (a Camaldolese, whom Dom Leclercq calls an arrant conservative) because he says my love of solitude is too much like Thoreau's. Hence my love for Thoreau is something that conservatives have against me.

One of the things I like best about Thoreau is not usually remarked on. It is the fact that he is something of a bridge builder between East and West. Gandhi liked his essay "Civil Disobedience," and Thoreau had a liking for Oriental philosophy. So do I. I have a book on that coming out this year [*Mystics and Zen Masters*], I hope. Thoreau, to my mind, expresses the real spirit of American personalism and freedom, the ability to be a non-conformist and to "listen to a different drummer." I remember now I have a line or two on him in my book *Conjectures of a Guilty Bystander,* which is a notebook, parts of which have appeared in *Harper's* and elsewhere, and which is slated to appear in the fall. Actually, though, I only quote something Emerson said of him.

That's about it. I wish I could have given you more. It is not that I have immersed myself in Thoreau, it is just that we are birds of a feather, I suppose.

(WTF 171)

From "Three Saviors in Camus," September 1966

THE WORK OF CAMUS is essentially meditative, imaginative, and symbolic. He constructs myths and images in which he elaborates his main themes. The awakening and clarification of the "lucid consciousness" is of course a matter of personal meditation: but it is much more than that. It depends most of all on the encounter and communion of persons. Camus frequently admits an attraction to solitude and silence—he had even read with approval Chateaubriand's life of Rancé, the seventeenth-century monastic reformer of La Trappe—but he always felt that this attraction was a mere temptation to be firmly resisted. He needed to be present among men, for his own sake as well as for theirs. He needed, with them, to develop a new and more human style of life in the absurdity of a world torn by a power struggle of immense magnitude. In the midst of this struggle it was the mission of a few men to preserve the purity of communication within a human measure and safeguard the clarity and sincerity of language in order that men might love. The "human task," he said, was "a humble and limited one: to find those few words by which to appease the infinite anguish of free souls." Of course he meant more than the phrase says by itself. He was concerned with the power of language—of truth then—to protect man against ferocity, murder, nihilism, chaos. Language used clearly and honestly in the service of a lucid consciousness would protect man against his tendencies to nihilism and self-destruction.

(LE 275–76)

• • •

So Camus, deeply concerned as he is with the loneliness and estrangement of man, is also preoccupied even more deeply still with the problem of communication. In his notebooks he writes, "Peace would be loving in silence. But there is conscience and the person; you have to speak. To love becomes hell." He has no naïve illusion that communication has become an easy matter in the age of TV. He is fully aware of its extreme difficulty, precisely because of the prevalence of sham communication and sham community. Curiously, in the next notebook entry he remarks on an actor who is a believer and who lies in bed listening to Mass on the radio. "No need to get up. He has salved his conscience." The great difficulty facing the man who really wants to communicate with his brother is not the lack of words or of media, but the fact that words and media are now so commonly and so systematically used in order to cheat and to lie.

(LE 276)

From "Ruben Dario." Fall 1996

A LL TRUE POETIC GENIUS tends to generate prophetic insight. The poet cannot help but listen to awakening voices that are not yet audible to the rest of men. The greatness of Ruben Dario lay not only in the orphic power of the song by which he transformed the Spanish poetry of his own time but also in the prophetic apprehension in which he foresaw something of our own age. While we salute the eloquence, the creative freedom, the luminosity, the passionate fervor of this great spirit, we must also pay attention to what he tells us about ourselves: and this we are less likely to expect of him, since *modernismo* is no longer modern but dated, like the *art nouveau* which was its contemporary. Yet even in his poetic style Ruben Dario had at his command a rich diversity of tone and harmony, and (if one may express a personal preference) his admirable "Sonnet to Cervantes," at once limpid, casual, and profound, anticipates the less rhetorical poetic tastes of a later generation.

Dario was concerned not only with poetic renewal but with man himself, and especially with the future of the two Americas. In the universality of his genius and in the strength of his poetic aspiration to unity, Ruben Dario longed for a world that would be culturally and spiritually one in civilized harmony and fraternal co-operation. But he foresaw the danger to this dream of unity—the danger of power used blindly by men of personal sincerity and limited understanding (not to mention the abuse of power by others less sincere and perhaps more intelligent). He foresaw the perils of an age that would set too great a price upon machines and muscles and too little upon authentic civilized and ethical values. He foresaw above all the terrible difficulties that would beset the vitally necessary dialogue between the two Americas: the Anglo-Saxon north and the Ibero-Indian south. Ruben Dario was fully aware of the importance of mutual understanding between these great racial and national complexes. He foresaw, too, that the dialogue between them could all too possibly remain superficial and might perhaps one day be silenced in a violent, inarticulate frenzy. One has only to recall his devastating poem to [Theodore] Roosevelt, the broncobuster, tiger killer, and "professor of energy." In the "language of the Bible and Whitman" Ruben Dario appealed not only to the president but to the whole North American people for a better understanding of the complexities and needs of their brothers in the South. In spite of many earnest gestures of goodwill and sincere efforts at understanding, we are permitted to wonder if the desired results have ever been attained, except in the case of a few exceptional men. It is to be regretted that North America never appreciated Ruben Dario as did Europe, and his voice has been only imperfectly heard here.

(LE 305–6)

From Conjectures of a Guilty Bystander, *1966*

JULIEN GREEN continually asks himself: can a novelist be a saint? Can a novelist save his soul? But perhaps the salvation of his soul depends precisely on his willingness to take that risk, and to be a novelist. And perhaps if he refused to challenge and accepted something that seemed to him more "safe," he would be lost. "He that will save his life must lose it."

(CGB 143)

From "The True Legendary Sound: The Poetry and Criticism of Edwin Muir," September 1966

THE POETRY OF EDWIN MUIR gives evidence of profound metaphysical concern: concern for the roots of being, for being in act, manifested by numinous and symbolic qualities. He does not seek these roots out of curiosity, nor does he find them in speculative and dialectical discussion. As a poet, Muir felt himself compelled to "divine and persuade"—to divine in the sense of a water-diviner finding hidden springs; to persuade, not by demonstration but by sharing the water with others.

(LE 29)

From "Prophetic Ambiguities: Milton and Camus," 1966

POETS AND POETIC THINKERS—men who construct myths in which they embody their own struggle to cope with the fundamental questions of life—are generally "prophetic" in the sense that they anticipate in their solitude the struggles and the general consciousness of later generations. Rereading Milton in the 1960s one cannot help realizing at once how close he is to us and how remote from us. He is remote, if you like, in his classic stamina— his capacity to develop his ideas in the longest and most noble periods. He is remote from us in his moral assumptions and his worldview. Yet the ideas and experiences he develops are often (not always) strikingly contemporary.

For instance his passionate concern with free speech in *Areopagitica*—an anti-Catholic tract if ever there was one—has borne fruit, through the effort of American Catholic bishops and theologians, in the Second Vatican Council's declaration on religious liberty. His concern with the dignity and liberty of the human person has now become everybody's cliché (though not everybody's dignity or liberty). As for *Paradise Lost,* without slandering the nobility of this great poem, we have to admit that there are times when it is structured like a movie or even like a comic strip. Milton sometimes has a very modern imagination. There are scenes in which Satan is Batman. More seriously, there are unquestionable affinities between Milton's Satan and the Superman not of the comics but of Nietzsche.

(LE 252)

From "Camus and the Church," December 1966

IN AN AGE of highly academic linguistic analysis, Camus appreciated the courage of [Brice] Parain, who sees the problem of language as ultimately a *metaphysical* problem. The questioning of meaning raises the whole question of reality itself and in the end Parain is asking one thing above all: can language make sense if there is no God? In other words, what is the point of talking about truth and falsity if there is no God? Is not man, in that case, reduced to putting together a series of more or less arbitrary noises in the solitude of a mute world? Are these noises anything more than the signals of animals and birds? True, our noises exist in a very complex ongoing context of development and are richly associated with one another and with other cultural phenomena: but can they be true? And does this matter?

Or, are they merely incidents in a developing adventure that will one day end in some kind of meaning but which, for the time being, has none?

Parain rejects this post-Hegelian position and returns to the classical ideas of language as able to provide grounds for at least elementary certitude. If language has no meaning then nothing has any meaning. Language has enough meaning, at least, to reassure us that we are not floating in a pure void. In other words, communication becomes possible, and with it community, once it is admitted that our words are capable of being true or false and that the decision is largely up to us. "To name a thing wrong is to add to the miseries of the world." We are thus called to take care of our language, and use it clearly. "The great task of man is not to serve the lie." These words of Parain might have been uttered—and have been uttered equivalently, many times—by Camus. And so Camus says in a review-article of Parain's books: "It is not altogether certain that our epoch has lacked gods: it seems on the contrary that what we need is a dictionary."

It is certainly true that the twentieth century has been distinguished for its single-minded adoration of political and cultural idols rather than for the clarity and honesty of its official speech. The sheer quantity of printed and broadcasted double-talk overwhelms the lucid utterances of a few men like Camus.

(LE 271–72)

From "The Plague *of Albert Camus*," *1967*

CAMUS IS SOMETIMES represented as having preached "the absurd." Nothing could be more mistaken. He wants his reader to recognize "the absurd" in order to resist it. "The absurd" is simply one face of "the plague" which we must resist in all its aspects. The Plague is the tyranny of evil and of death, no matter what form it may take: the Nazi occupation of France, the death camps, the bourgeois hypocrisy of the French system (which Camus had observed in action in the colony of Algeria), Stalinism, or the unprincipled opportunism of certain French Marxists. All such types uneasily sensed that *The Plague* was talking about them—and we might add that the same Plague is not absent from the United States today.

(LE 182)

• • •

The lucid realization of the absurd is, for Camus, only a first step. The function of this lucidity is not simply to negate and to deride the illusory standards of bourgeois society. Still less is it merely a groundwork for an ethic of austere and ironic despair. It is the first step toward a kind of modest hope. *The Myth of Sisyphus* is explicitly directed against suicide. Where one might be tempted to think "because life is absurd, let's get it over with," Camus replies, "because life is absurd that is all the more reason for living, and for refusing to surrender to its absurdity."

Life then becomes a revolt against negation, unhappiness, and inevitable death. It is, under these conditions of lucidity and courage, a valid affirmation of freedom: the only freedom man has, the freedom to keep going even though a certain logic might seem to prove that resistance is useless. Camus detects this logic subtly at work in society itself and in the apparent "order" and "truth" by which society lives.

(LE 197)

• • •

Camus, without knowing it, was in the thick of the old argument of grace versus the law and, without being aware of the fact, was on the side of grace. He found himself disputing in grace's favor against those who had turned grace into a purely arbitrary law. This is not to say that Camus was a secret Christian, but only that a Christian is free, if he likes, to understand Camus in a Christian sense which Camus himself did not realize.

(LE 202)

From "Camus: Journals of the Plague Years," 1967

THE SITUATION OF twentieth-century man is absurd (Camus believes) because it consistently forces him into radical self-contradiction. The final idiocy to which complacent modern man is tempted consists in using all his resources of logic and of science to demonstrate that his self-contradictions make perfect sense. Camus refuses to consent to this gigantic hoax, and decides that if there is a meaning to be found in life it must be sought in revolt, in resistance against the plague, the kind of heroic and seemingly hopeless resistance which he and his fellow-countrymen put up against overwhelming odds during World War II.

It was in this resistance that Camus, as editor of a clandestine resistance newspaper, *Combat,* learned the seriousness of words. When you realize that you may be shot for your editorial, he said, you weigh what you say. You make sure you mean it.

(LE 220)

From a Letter to Mario Falsina, March 25, 1967

Mario Falsina was a student at the Catholic University of the Sacred Heart in Milan, Italy. He was writing a thesis on Merton.

EUROPEAN AND AMERICAN thinkers who have influenced me. Religious: St. Thomas Aquinas (well, he is Italian too really), Duns Scotus, St. Augustine, St. Gregory the Great, St. Bernard. Mystics: Tauler, Ruysbroeck, St. John of the Cross, St. Theresa, St. Thérèse. Modern theological writers: Hans von Balthasar, [Henri] De Lubac, [Jean] Daniélou, [Louis] Bouyer, Dom Leclercq, K. Rahner, Romano Guardini, Jacques Maritain, É. Gilson. Others: Pascal, Shakespeare, Blake, T. S. Eliot, Rilke, Dostoevsky, [Nikolai] Berdyaev, Joyce, Camus, Graham Greene, Léon Bloy, René Char, St. John Perse. Americans: Thoreau, Faulkner, William Carlos Williams, Mark Van Doren, Emily Dickinson. Some others: F. García Lorca, César Vallejo, Aldous Huxley. I have obviously forgotten some important ones, but that is the best I can do now.

(RTJ 349)

From "Faulkner and His Critics," April–May 1967

FAULKNER WAS AN OUTRAGEOUSLY and deliberately demanding writer. His tortuously involved time sequences, his interminable sentences, his multiplication of characters with the same name in the same book had one purpose above all: to ensure that the reader either became involved in the book or else dropped it altogether. Yet it is obvious, too, that Faulkner's style was often self-defeating.

If it involved the reader enough to make him go back over a thirty-line sentence to puzzle out its meaning, and if after that the reader found the thirty-line sentence did not matter anyway, he would be likely to regret his involvement and throw the book aside. Faulkner's long sentences are perhaps meant more to obsess than to enlighten. But in any event involvement in Faulkner means something more than paying close attention to a story: it means entering into the power of his mythical obsessions. In the words of the French critic Claude-Edmonde Magny, it means allowing Faulkner to cast his spells over you: for in her opinion Faulkner works like a prehistoric shaman who enmeshes the reader in numinous symbols and entrances him with sacred horror. To quote Conrad, the reader gets the feeling of "being captured by the incredible which is the very essence of dreams."

Unfortunately, there is a certain type of mind which fears and avoids this kind of witchery. The thing is dangerous. Too much is let loose. The spells are too awful. And there are various ways of defending oneself against them. The obvious refusal of assent is typified by the easy ridicule which Fadiman poured on Sutpen in *Absalom.* "He's the fellow you're supposed to shudder at, and if you understand Mr. Faulkner you'll shudder."

The only really serious Faulkner criticism is that which assents to the myth firmly enough to be captured by the incredible and then judges it from within: is it authentic, or phony? In between these two poles, of mere ridicule and serious involvement, is what one might call the standard American objection to Faulkner: the repudiation of an apocalyptic mystique of the absurd, which is Faulkner's way of celebrating the American destiny.

(LE 118–19)

From a Letter to Scott Wright,
May 26, 1967

Scott Wright was a student getting a masters degree in literary science from the University of Michigan. As part of his degree program, he wrote an essay on Merton and Norman Mailer.

T HANKS FOR YOUR LETTER and for your essay on "The Merton-Mailer Vision." I am not surprised at your approach. I have not read a great deal of Mailer but what I have read not only interests me but strikes the right chord, I think. We do have something of the same kind of protest to utter, in our different ways. Besides that, someone [Michele Murray, "Life Viewed Too Facilely"] criticizing *Conjectures* in a Catholic paper, held this against me that I was "like Norman Mailer" (*National Catholic Reporter,* early this year sometime). I'll see if I can dig up a copy of the letter I wrote to the paper ["Thomas Merton Replies to a Perceptive Critic"] accepting this not as a stigma but as something that seemed to be reasonable. Like Mailer, I am not able to agree with a completely square and sociological sort of liberalism which really accepts the suburban and technological thing just as it is, and wants only more of the same. Unfortunately this is what passes for advanced thinking among many Catholics since the Council. They imagine that this is what it means to understand the "modern world." I'll send a copy of an essay that has something to do with this, if I can find it. I am grateful for your thoughtfulness. Did you send a copy to Mailer? In any event, your essay is a reminder for me to go and read those things of his that I have not read (most of his books). I also like James Baldwin, as you know.

(RTJ 353)

From a letter to Nancy Fly Bredenberg, December 11, 1967

Nancy Fly Bredenberg was at Vassar College and study-ing with David Ignatow.

D ENISE LEVERTOV was here yesterday and in our good visit together I was reminded of Vassar and thought of your letter. I'd better try to answer it while it is still in my mind. I can't really give you a lot of details, but anyhow I'll try to say something.

First, I am glad you like my poems. It is always nice to have readers who are attuned to what you are trying to say. I don't write in a pure void, and though I am not very much concerned about stature publishing, I am glad to reach readers and especially young ones. I guess most of the readers of my poetry are young. At least they are the ones who seem to respond most. I am happy about that.

I would say that I don't belong with any of the groups or schools, and am certainly not involved in the petty or-thodoxies of this and that school.

What poets do I like? I am very fond of some Spanish and Latin American poetry, more than what is written in the States. But of North American poets, well, my favorite is [Louis] Zukofsky. I do like Bill Williams [William Car-los Williams] but I find I don't read a great deal of him. [Ezra] Pound I respect and don't read. [Robert] Duncan I like. [George] Oppen I have quoted some. [Robert] Creely etc. OK. I wouldn't say any of these had influenced me. Denise Levertov I respond to very much as a poet and a person. But myself I think I am more subject to European and Latin American influences. Vallejo is perhaps the twentieth century poet who means most to me. And Lorca did a long time ago, still does I guess. Rilke. Eliot. Dylan

Thomas. One of the most exciting poets writing today in my opinion is Peter Levi. And in French, René Char: great, great stuff. And I like Neruda. Octavio Paz, etc.

Writing means a great deal to me but I am, as I say, rather out of the literary world, at least the orthodox and competitive literary world. But I have friends in it here and there and all around. Oh, another American poet I like very much and really admire, is Ronald Johnson. Very fine! I'm not nuts about [Charles] Olson, so like Jackson Mac Low etc. I could just write a lot of etc's after that. Some magazines I do see sometimes, others never. Criticism: I don't see much of it and I don't get the impression that I come in for much attention one way or the other. Some of the criticism of my stuff seems to me huffy and square: the thing that gets people most mad at me is a certain world-denying protest against the supermarket culture, but this is silly and it is only one aspect of my work anyhow. Probably too my Christian and eschatological bent bothers a certain type of academic: but I am certainly not a regular "Catholic poet" in any establishment sense. Far from it! The Catlicks too regard me as something of a maverick, except in the early "spiritual writing." Well, I'll slip a few papers in this that may help, as I have to stop now. Best wishes to you, and I hope your paper comes out all right.

(RTJ 361–62)

From *"The Answer of Minerva: Pacifism and Resistance in Simone Weil,"* 1968

LIKE BERNANOS AND CAMUS, Simone Weil is one of those brilliant and independent French thinkers who were able to articulate the deepest concerns of France and Europe in the first half of this century. More controversial and perhaps more of a genius than the others, harder to situate, she has been called all kinds of names, both good and bad and often contradictory: Gnostic and Catholic, Jew and Albigensian, medievalist and modernist, Platonist and anarchist, rebel and saint, rationalist and mystic. De Gaulle said he thought she was out of her mind. The doctor in the sanatorium at Ashford, Kent, where she died (August 24, 1943) said, "She had a curious religious outlook and (probably) no religion at all." In any case, whatever is said about her, she can always be treated as "an enigma." Which is simply to say that she is somewhat more difficult to categorize than most people, since in her passion for integrity she absolutely refused to take up any position she had not first thought out in the light of what she believed to be a personal vocation to "absolute intellectual honesty." When she began to examine any accepted position, she easily detected its weaknesses and inconsistencies.

(NVA 144)

• • •

For us (since we imagine that we have no myths at all), myth actually is without limitation and can easily penetrate the whole realm of political, social, and ethical thought. Thus, instead of going to war because the gods have been arguing among themselves, we go because of "secret plots" and sinister combinations, because of political slogans elevated to the dignity of metaphysical absolutes: "Our political universe is peopled with myths and monsters—we know nothing there but absolutes." We shed blood for high-sounding words spelled out in capital letters. We seek to impart content to them by destroying other men who believe in enemy-words, also in capital letters.

But how can men really be brought to kill each other for what is objectively void? The nothingness of national, class, or racial myth must receive an apparent substance, not from intelligible content but from the *will to destroy and be destroyed.* (We may observe here that the substance of idolatry is the willingness to give reality to metaphysical nothingness by sacrificing to it. The more totally one destroys present realities and alienates oneself to an object which is really void, the more total is the idolatry, i.e., the commitment to the falsehood that the non-entity is an objective absolute. Note here that in this context the God of the mystics is not "an object" and cannot be described properly as "an entity" among other entities. Hence one of the marks of authentic mysticism is that God as experienced by the mystic can in no way be the object of an idolatrous cult.)

(NVA 147)

From *"A Footnote from* Ulysses: *Peace and Revolution,"* 1968

ONE OF THE MAIN themes of *Ulysses* is the breakdown of language and of communication as part of the disruption of Western culture. The extraordinary linguistic richness of the book—which, however, comes out mostly in parody—only reminds us more forcefully how much further the breakdown has gone in the last fifty years. Pacifism and nonviolence are fully and consciously involved in this question of language. Nonviolence, as Gandhi conceived it, is in fact a kind of language. The real dynamic of nonviolence can be considered as a purification of language, a restoration of true communication on a human level, when language has been emptied of meaning by misuse and corruption. Nonviolence is meant to communicate love not in word but in act. Above all, nonviolence is meant to convey and to defend truth which has been obscured and defiled by political double-talk.

The real lesson of all this for us is this: we must clearly understand the function of nonviolence against the background of the collapse of language.

(LE 27)

From "News of the Joyce Industry," 1968

THE VERY ESSENCE of comic art—the stasis of comic "joy," as Joyce himself might have said—is found in the living balance, the poise between vital uncertainties and unanswered questions which constitute, for a classic temper, the authentic mystery of life. The moral and cultural death which Joyce found so stifling in the Dublin of 1904 consisted precisely in this mania for prescription and foreclosure, this fanatic closing of doors and throwing away of keys, this craze for decreeing that all problems are hereby solved and all the questions answered. Consider the soliloquy of Father Conmee, S.J., in the "wandering rocks" section of *Ulysses*. Consider Bloom himself, whom critics tend more and more to treat as a real hero rather than a mock heroic figure: one of his comic features is that he has at least a provisional answer for everything. He finds an instant name for everything, locates it, pigeonholes it in an alienated experience that is one huge inexhaustible cliché. (And critics pore over these pathetic thrusts as if they were keys to all philosophy and all history!) Now the main problem of the Joyce industry is that it tends to reward scholars for ignoring and destroying this delicate balance. They are encouraged, by the rules of their game, to espouse one contradiction against the other, to choose between polarized energies, to decree that the "real Joyce" must be situated on one pole or the other, not in the tension between them.

(LE 15)

From "Blake and the New Theology," 1968

BLAKE, LIKE [HERBERT] MARCUSE after him, recognized the two-dimensional character of Western logic and also the endemic temptation to reduce this tension to a one-dimensional and authoritarian system. The ideological tension between "what is" and "what ought to be" is at the heart of the experience of fallenness, which should, in Gospel terms, open out in need for redemption. But it is also characteristic of fallenness that it evades this need and this tension by substituting an artificial and rigid one-dimensional "order." This falsification can be canonized and perpetuated by the "laws" of a frozen, authoritarian system, and the "god" who presides over such a system is at once a "nothing" and an absolute power, Urizen, the Negation, the "Abstract objecting power that Negatives everything / . . . the Spectre of Man . . . / And in its Holiness is closed the Abomination of Desolation" ("Jerusalem"). True holiness and redemption, for Blake, lie in the energy that springs from the reunion of Contraries. But the Negation stands between the Contraries and prevents their "marriage." Holding heaven and hell apart, Urizen infects them both with his own sickness and nothingness. True holiness, faith, vision, Christianity, must therefore subvert his power to Negate and "redeem the contraries" in mercy, pity, peace. The work of this reversal is the epiphany of God in Man. The God that "is dead" is therefore the Negation set up in solitary and absolute authority as an idol and Spectre. But this God is endowed with life in proportion as men invest him with (earthly) power and adore him in his separateness and isolation— even putting one another to death in his honor. The beginning of faith must obviously be a "no" to this idol, this

Negation of life and of love. But the negation of the Negation and the restoration of Contraries is not just the work of the intelligence. In Blake it was, and had to be, a mystical and prophetic experience involving the whole man.

(LE 7)

On His Own Writing

I N RETURNING THE NOVEL (*The Labyrinth*), Farrar and Rinehart announced they were not enthusiastic enough about it to publish it. Trying to find out more, I repeatedly got on the telephone, and talked to a woman whose job it is to say "we never discuss refused manuscripts." Then, quite by chance, she suddenly relented, half hoping I would not turn out to be a maniac after all, and let me talk to a man who had not read the novel, but whom, at any rate, I saw. From the notes of one who *had* read it, he told me the story was impossible to follow, and shoddily written. That it often got dull and boring. That this man had not bothered to finish it. That the names of the characters were ugly and disconcerting, and the characters themselves were unreal.

Looking at the thing again, I find all that is true. He said it was obvious enough I wanted to write a novel, and that it showed promise. I believed that in the first place.

He asked: what was I trying to do, create some utterly new kind of novel structure? The name of Joyce slipped into one of his sentences, intimating that sort of thing was all right, perhaps, in Joyce. I hastened to deny that I was striving after originality. That is, originality for its own sake, and apart from the novel.

Coming home I rearranged all the chapters in a different order, and now I haven't any idea what to do with the thing. That was Thursday.

(RUN 50–51)

Journal Entry, October 22, Sunday, 1939

IF I HAD MORE HUMILITY and did not rush to write things down so fast, and did not assume that everything is interesting if you put it in writing I would make fewer crazy statements and say some things so that they are as true as I see them. But what presumption, when I know nothing about philosophy—know so little about it that I can't even read it carefully. But anyway, I do not aspire to be a philosopher—but go after allegorical theology which is not argumentative: but there: I am not sure what allegorical theology *is,* but only know one thing it is *not.* And that thing—argumentativeness: well I am always obviously trying to be argumentative. Perhaps I had better not argue with myself anymore about the validity of writing things down in this book. All right: it is not for reading: and the embarrassment of reading some of the stuff over again comes under the heading of mortification of pride.

(RUN 62)

From a Letter to Robert Lax, February 4, 1940

I TOOK THE NOVEL TO MACMILLANS. I got it back just the other day. Mr. Purdy who is their manager is a good guy. He give me a long letter saying the readers had told him it was a pretty good book all right, only it ought to be boiled down and changed etc. He quoted one of the readers' reports saying the characters were copied from Hemingway and the writing was copied from Joyce and I myself sounded like a smart fellow only the reader wisht I didn't argue so much about religion in the book.

So just last week I ripped out all the pages of argument about anything that I could find (that was plenty of pages) and sent the book to Harcourt Brace. I have been trying to figure out why that reader thought the characters were copied from Hemingway. Now that pages and pages of meditation have been torn out and thrown away I hope nobody will be sore at the book, but on the contrary print it right away. I wisht I knew. I wisht I really cared, too, as a matter of fact.

(WHEN 42)

From The Seven Storey Mountain, *1948*

WHEN I LIVED ON PERRY STREET, it was hard to write poems. The lines came slow, and when it was all done, there were very few of them. They were generally rhymed iambic tetrameter, and because I was uneasy with any rhyme that sounded hackneyed, rhyming was awkward and sometimes strange.

I would get an idea, and walk around the streets, among the warehouses, towards the poultry market at the foot of Twelfth Street, and I would go out on the chicken dock trying to work out four lines of verse in my head, and sit in the sun. And after I had looked at the fireboats and the old empty barges and the other loafers and the Stevens Institute on its bluff across the river in Hoboken, I would write the poem down on a piece of scrap paper and go home and type it out.

I usually sent it at once to some magazine. How many envelopes I fed to the green mailbox at the corner of Perry Street just before you got to Seventh Avenue! And everything I put in there came back—except for the book reviews.

The more I failed, the more I was convinced that it was important for me to have my work printed in magazines like the *Southern Review* or *Partisan Review* or the *New Yorker*. My chief concern was now to see myself in print. It was as if I could not be quite satisfied that I was real until I could feed my ambition with these trivial glories, and my ancient selfishness was now matured and concentrated in this desire to see myself externalized in a public and printed and official self which I could admire at my ease. This was what I really believed in: reputation, success. I wanted to live in the eyes and the mouths and the minds of men. I was not so crude that I wanted to be known and admired by the whole world: There was a certain naive satisfaction in the idea of being only appreciated by a particular minority, which gave a special fascination to this urge within me. But when my mind was absorbed in that, how could I lead a supernatural life, the life to which I was called? How could I love God when everything I did was done not for Him but for myself, and not trusting in His aid, but relying on my own talents?

(SSM 236)

• • •

In the gay days of early June, in the time of examinations, I was beginning a new book. It was called *The Journal of My Escape from the Nazis* and it was the kind of book that I liked to write, full of double-talk and all kinds of fancy ideas that sounded like Franz Kafka. One reason why it was satisfying was that it fulfilled a kind of psychological necessity that had been pent up in me all through the last stages of the war because of my sense of identification, by guilt, with what was going on in England.

So I put myself there and, telescoping my own past with the air raids that were actually taking place, as its result, I wrote this journal. And, as I say, it was something I needed to write, although I often went off at a tangent, and the thing got away up more than one blind alley.

And so, absorbed in this work, and in the final examinations, and in preparation for the coming summer school, I let the question of the Trappist vocation drop into the background, although I could not drop it altogether.

I said to myself: after summer school, I will go and make a retreat with the Trappists in Canada, at Our Lady of the Lake, outside Montreal.

(SSM 336)

From a Letter to Evelyn Waugh, August 2, 1948

Waugh was a celebrated British novelist, author of The Loved One *and* Brideshead Revisited. *He edited the British version of* The Seven Storey Mountain, *titled* Elected Silence.

T HE REAL REASON I WRITE TO YOU is not merely to rehash these little details. I am in a difficult spot here as a writer. Father Abbot gives me a typewriter and says "write" and so I cover pages and pages with matter and they go to several different censors and get lost, torn up, burned, and so on. Then they get pieced together and retyped and go to a publisher who changes everything and after about four years a book appears in print. I never get a chance to discuss it with anybody and scarcely ever see any reviews and half the time I haven't the faintest idea whether the thing is good or bad or what it is. Therefore I need criticism the way a man dying of thirst needs water. Those who have any ideas in their head about writing and who can communicate with me by letter or word have so far told me that I need discipline. I know. But I don't *get* it. A man can do something for himself along those lines by paying attention and using his head, I suppose. But if you can offer me any suggestions, tell me anything I ought to read, or tell me in one or two sentences how I ought to comport myself to acquire discipline, I would be immensely grateful and you would be doing something for my soul. Because this business of writing has become intimately tied up with the whole process of my sanctification. It is an ascetic matter as much as anything else, because of the peculiar circumstances under which I write. At the moment, I may add, I am faced with a program of much writing because we have to raise money to build some new monasteries and there is a flood of vocations. Most of what I have to do concerns the Cistercian life, history, spiritual theology, biographies etc. But (be patient with me!), consider this problem: all this has suddenly piled up on me in the last two years and I find myself more or less morally obliged to continue connections with the most diverse kind of publishers. On one end of the dilemma I am writing poetry and things like that for New Directions and a wacky surrealist magazine called *Tiger's Eye* that I think I had better get out of.

(CFT 4–5)

From a Letter to Jacques Maritain, February 10, 1949

I AM SWAMPED WITH WORK. I am trying very hard to break the ground on a book on the contemplative life. It is the first try I have had at sustained theology, and I find the going rather difficult, besides which I am being constantly interrupted. I rather think Our Lord is blocking the book for the time being because He sees that it will be better later on. But really, as Sertillanges says, the life of a writer can be very grueling, and I do not hesitate to say that the severest penances I have experienced here as a Cistercian have all had to do with trying to get ideas down on paper. To be a theologian demands a severe interior asceticism, and when I find myself sighing for a life of simplicity and solitude and obscurity I wonder if, after all, I am not just seeking luxury. The other day we had the life of St. Benedict Joseph Labre in the refectory and, as usual, I came out with thoughts of myself enjoying the abjection of one despised by all etc. etc. . . . But afterwards I was forced to admit that for me sanctity is quite probably connected with books and with writing and intellectual drudgery. On the whole it is probably easier to be a tramp than a scholar.

(CFT 24)

Journal Entry, April 29, 1949, Feast of Saint Robert

IT IS EXTREMELY DIFFICULT to write theology well. The main reason why I can write it is that I don't know it. I don't know precisely what I mean to say and therefore when I start to write, I find that I am working out a theory as I go. And I get into the most terrible confusion, saying things which I try to explain—to myself more than to anyone else—and rambling off the track of the plan I had arranged.

I wonder how many plans I have made for this book, *The School of the Spirit?* Perhaps six—including the ones I made for it when it was called *The Cloud and the Fire*. So I sit at the typewriter with my fingers all wound up in a cat's cradle of strings, overwhelmed with the sense of my own stupidity and surrounded by not one but many literary dilemmas.

I am supposed now to be working on the book three afternoons a week and try at all costs to get something down on paper, terrified that if I merely stop and read and organize notes, I will go around in circles forever and ever. This business of "getting my notes together" is something that can go on absolutely interminably, because there exists an almost unlimited number of combinations in which you can arrange the statements you have jotted down so carefully on some eight hundred pages of various notebooks.

All that undigested material is utterly terrifying and fascinating at the same time. Sometimes I try to "meditate" on this monster which I call "my notes." (I should say "our" notes, but skip it.) But the statements standing—out of context and in my own crazy handwriting—do not have the meaning and unction they had in [Jacque-Paul] Migne or St. John of the Cross or wherever I first read them. . . .

They seem to divide and slacken my mind and leave my spirit in a *vague* state of perturbation at the thought that I have eaten the Fathers and produced nothing but this unhappy web.

But when I tell myself, "I am no writer, I am finished," instead of being upset I am filled with a sense of peace and of relief, perhaps because I already taste, by anticipation, the joy of my deliverance. On the other hand, if I am not delivered from writing by failure, perhaps I may go on and even succeed at this thing, but by the power of the Holy Ghost—which would be a greater deliverance. But whatever happens, success or failure, I have given up worrying. I just wonder about the business on paper, on the assumption that it might mean something to me if I should ever reread all this at another season.

(SOJ 178–79)

Journal Entry, July 10, 1949

I AM GLAD THE BOOK [*Seeds of Contemplation*] has been written and read [aloud in the monastery rectory at mealtime]. Surely I have said enough about the business of darkness and about the "experimental contact with God in obscurity" to be able to shut up about it and go on to something else for a change. Otherwise it will just get to be mechanical—grinding out the same old sot over and over again. But if it had not been read aloud at me, I might have forgotten how often I had said all those things, and gone on saying them again as if they were discoveries. For I am aware that this often happens in our life. Keeping a journal has taught me that there is not so much new in the interior life as one sometimes thinks. When you reread your journal you find out that your newest discovery is something you already found out five years ago. Still, it is true that one penetrates deeper and deeper into the same ideas and the same experiences.

(ETS 333)

From a Letter to Sister Therese Lentfoehr, SDS, May, 6, 1950

DID YOU REVIEW the St. Lutgarde book [*What Are These Wounds?*]? I suppose you were your usual kind self, with a blind eye for all the stupidities in the thing. It is really badly done, this time, and we tried to persuade Bruce at any price not to publish it, but it was too late. I believe Our Lord permitted this in order to detach me from any conceit about myself as a writer. The sales of the other books have dropped tremendously since *Wounds* appeared: the book is just wrong for the non-Catholic reader in this country. Our Lord will take care of their souls. And if this puts a rift between me and the public, so much the better. That is just what there should be between a Cistercian and the public.

(RTJ 202)

Journal Entry, June 13, 1951

THE MAN WHO BEGAN this journal is dead, just as the man who finished *The Seven Storey Mountain* when this journal began was also dead, and what is more the man who was the central figure in *The Seven Storey Mountain* was dead over and over. And now that all these men are dead, it is sufficient for me to say so on paper and I think I will have ended up by forgetting them. Because writing down what *The Seven Storey Mountain* was about was sufficient to get it off my mind for good. Last week I corrected the proofs of the French translation of the book and it seemed completely alien. I might as well have been a proofreader working for a publisher and going over the galleys of somebody else's book. Consequently, *The Seven Storey*

Mountain is the work of a man I never even heard of. And this journal is getting to be the production of somebody to whom I have never had the dishonor of an introduction.

(SOJ 328)

From a Letter to Étienne Gilson, November 12, 1951

Gilson (1884–1978), a major Catholic scholar, is the author of The Spirit of Medieval Philosophy, *which Merton first read while a student at Columbia.*

WHAT GREATER THING can we have than to be empty, to be despoiled, to be orphans and exiles in this world? Your exile is not merely metaphorical. It is something you suffer and offer to God for the France He loves and which nevertheless tends to reject Him and those whom He sends.

Thank you for the kind words you say about *The Ascent to Truth.* In none of the books that I have written do I feel that I have said what I wanted. I do not know whether or not in this one I have said what needs to be said to any except a few. I have the consciousness of having disappointed many who wanted me to say something to *them.* Also I have an even greater consciousness that I have nothing to say to anyone except the oaks of our forest. Like St. Bernard, I feel that I can go to them and learn everything. I dare not say that like him I feel like the chimera of the age, lest it suggest a sort of comparison between an unworthy son and so great a Father—and this is a comparison which I cannot afford to make.

(SOC 31)

From a Letter to Dom Gabriel Sortais, February 1953

1. Is it your will that I don't write *anymore* a *single* book?

2. Or do you want me not to write a book while I am Student Master?

3. Do you allow the eventual publication of the conferences given to the students, and of the main ideas of their formation? All the same I must write them [for the students], and I get them photocopied. So it is a more or less unavoidable *work*.

4. Or, apart from the journal and every autobiographical and formally "personal" narrative, would you allow a book provided it does not hinder the interior life and does not disagree with our monastic ideal—e.g., meditations, studies on the interior life, lives of saints, studies in Holy Scripture, etc.?

In principle, my Most Reverend Father, any work as a writer should be for us *rare and exceptional.* If you want to know what I frankly think, before God, in my own case, I will tell you this: what I find most embarrassing is to try to do a scholar's job, to speak as an historian, a dogmatic theologian, etc. I also have more or less given up writing as a *poet,* but sometimes an idea may come, it gets written, so to speak, of its own accord, and it helps to *deepen some insight* about God, about the spiritual life, etc. Also fragments of meditations, *impersonal and objective,* upon the truths of faith, our relations with God. It is these fragments (in the line of *Seeds of Contemplation*) that seem to me to be our affair, if we write anything at all. But if I must go on working along this line it will remain, for me, as for the others, *rare and exceptional*!

I ask you these questions with simplicity, precisely to know where I must direct our efforts. A few years ago, with Dom James' approval, I signed a contract with our editor [Robert Giroux] aiming at the publication of four books of which one has been delivered [*The Ascent to Truth,* 1953]. The others were to be a life of Saint Aelred [not completed], a book on Saint Bernard [*The Last of the Fathers,* 1954], a book on the Holy Mass [unwritten]. I assure you I have very little taste for these works, all of which seem to demand a little erudition. There remains the fact that I am under an obligation of providing him (the publisher) with three more books.

Besides, I *am* convinced of the truthfulness of what you say about the dangers of a writer's life. One may think one has very pure intentions, but publicity is an altogether nefarious thing which seduces us in spite of ourselves. Also the preoccupations of success, of the diffusion of the book, etc. I have resisted them with all my strength, but I am sure I have not avoided being wounded many times.

(SOC 54–55)

From a Letter to Dom Jean Leclercq, July 28, 1954

I FEEL MUCH MORE GRATIFIED about being a writer now that I see that I can help other authentic testimonies of the monastic spirit to appear. I shall do everything I can to let you have another book, in order to help your series. Please tell your good Father Abbot that I feel that I am really doing the work of God in collaborating as much as I can with your series, and will feel that my own writing is thereby inserted in a truly monastic context. There is a special satisfaction in collaborating with one's brothers in

Christ, and I do not like the idea of an isolated and spectac-ular apostolate. No doubt I must have the courage to face the enemies that this isolation makes for me—even among priests and religious. But for my own part I prefer to be a member of a team, at least to some extent, than to be a soloist exclusively. However, since God has singled me out for a kind of isolation, I will certainly accept it, together with its consequences. That is certainly nothing new in the Church.

(SOC 78)

From a Letter to Dom Jean Leclercq, August 11, 1955

I HAVE STOPPED WRITING, and that is a big relief. I intend to renounce it for good, if I can live in solitude. I realize that I have perhaps suffered more than I knew from this "writing career." Writing is deep in my nature, and I can-not deceive myself that it will be very easy for me to do without it. At least I can get along without the public and without my reputation! Those are not essentially con-nected with the writing instinct. But the whole business tends to corrupt the purity of one's spirit of faith. It ob-scures the clarity of one's view of God and of divine things. It vitiates one's sense of spiritual reality, for as long as one imagines himself to be accomplishing something, he tends to become rich in his own eyes. But we must be poor, and live by God alone—whether we write or whatever else we may do. The time has come for me to enter more deeply into that poverty.

(SOC 89–90)

From a Letter to Dom Gabriel Sortais, February 7, 1957

*Sortais was one of Merton's principal "censors." A distin-
guished Cistercian, he had a colorful career before joining
the Trappists. He was captured by the Germans while
serving as a chaplain in the French army during World
War II and spent time in a prison camp.*

I AM TRYING to be a monk.

I am not writing and I do not think of writing anything whatsoever. True, I still have two or three manuscripts that are going to be published, but after that the
name of Thomas Merton can be forgotten. So much the
better. I continue to seek God through the somewhat
strange and solitary path that is mine. More and more I try
to pay no attention to myself. I know that I am in God's
hands and that I cannot see what He is in the process of
doing. Please bless me. I am sorry for all these problems,
Most Reverend Father; fortunately it will be all over soon.
I remain devotedly and loyally one with you in our Lord.

(SOC 101)

From a Letter to Czeslaw Milosz, September 12, 1959

I STILL DO NOT SHARE your scruples about writing,
though lately I have been thinking of giving it up for a
while, and seeking a more austere and solitary kind of existence (I go through that cycle frequently, as you have seen
in *The Sign of Jonas,* but this time it is more serious). I will
probably never give up writing definitively. I have just
been finishing another book, *The Inner Experience*—a

wider deeper view of the same thing, contemplation, with more reference to Oriental ideas. There is to me nothing but this that counts, but everything can enter into it. You are right to feel a certain shame about writing. I do too, but always too late—five years after a book has appeared I wish I had never been such a fool as to write it. But when I am writing it I think it is good. If we were not all fools, we would never accomplish anything at all.

(CFT 63)

From a Letter to Jaime Andrade, November 20, 1958

Andrade was an sculptor from Quito, Ecuador.

At present I have my hands full simply thinking my way into the clarity of an unconventional position and standing by it, resisting the powerful appeals of the massive groups and their authoritarian philosophies, and their sinister claims to be right because they are powerful and massive. Yet I know in the depths of my being that this is what we have to resist with every fiber and every nerve and every breath that is in us. The massive, powerful groups are *not* right. Even the Church is right only insofar as she preserves, behind the façade of power and authority, the humility and poverty of Christ: and this humility and poverty often have very little to do with the façade. Nothing at all. And those who cling to the Church because of her façade sometimes have nothing of her true inner reality.

It follows as a most bitter consequence of this that one must ever run the risk of being thought wrong, of being thought evil and misguided, not only by the powerful community "church" but even of being thought a bad Christian and a rebel by other Christians. I do not say by the Church, because I have no intention of getting myself officially condemned. But I must certainly expect to be attacked and vilified by theologians and by certain of the clergy—as Maritain, for example, has been attacked by the Falangists in unanimous chorus.

(SOC 114)

From a Letter to Dom Gabriel Sortais, January 26, 1959

I LEAVE THE JUDGMENT TO YOU, but it seems to me that I have a very serious duty to complete my article on Pasternak and to put the whole truth on paper. And to publish it. It is a question of giving a Christian explanation of Pasternak's witness which is both heroic and Christian. This affair has moved the hearts of everyone, but most profoundly it has touched those who are writers and intellectuals. It is about an event that has happened in the very midst of the spiritual life of our time. To dissociate myself from involvement with this action which is so extraordinary would be for me a betrayal: a betrayal of my particular vocation, a betrayal of Jesus Christ. At least this is the way I feel.

So as not to involve the Order in this event, I would be quite content to be allowed to publish an article under a pen name. Of course this would deprive the article of a good deal of its power as a Christian witness on Pasternak's behalf. But if you are unwilling to let me publish this article under my own name (and I beg you to let me do so), then at least permit me to publish it incognito. The secret could be very easily kept, since no one would expect such a document from a Trappist. But at the same time, if

I published it under my own name, people would hardly be shocked, because it is more or less known that I am a friend of Pasternak.

You know that I submit myself entirely to holy Obedience. I implore you to listen to me, Most Reverend Father; but if you believe that this project is out of the question, I submit myself to your judgment and God will not regard me as a traitor to my conscience. But I beg you on my knees at least to let me publish this report under a pen name.

(SOC 118)

From a Letter to Dom Gabriel Sortais, *May 21, 1960*

ONLY TODAY HAS DOM JAMES, back from his regular visits, handed me your observations on the censorship of the "Notes for a Philosophy of Solitude." If I had known what you thought about it in all earnestness I would never have written you a letter like that of the other day, which must have appeared to you altogether carefree, ironical even, maybe even rebellious. I have too much pain in writing you now to want to make useless explanations. What I tell you is a fully serious admission, which comes from the bottom of the heart with sincerity.

I have the impression of what it must feel like for a sick person who thinks he simply has a cold to discover suddenly that he has tuberculosis. I don't have the temptation to ask myself if the physician is mistaken. The diagnosis is too serious. The case is urgent.

I am going first to make scrupulously all the corrections that the censor asks of me. I am going to change what displeases you in the article on Mount Athos, without it having been asked of me. I change this not simply because you don't like it, but because I am wrong in speaking in this way. I am wrong in speaking without prudence, and in giving such painful impressions. I spoke like a fool: I am a fool, I am an idiot.

I am going to change not only the passages pointed out in the article on solitude, but *all* that might give an impression of scurrility, levity, lack of respect for the Church and for the Superiors. I was wrong in thinking that it sufficed to obey promptly when asked to do so, and in not thinking more seriously of the effect of my interior attitudes. I do not ask you to think that I am not malicious. You are a Father, so you must know it. For my part, I must accept the responsibility for my imprudent writings. I confess that I attach too much importance to my subjective sentiment of having goodwill. Goodwill does not suffice. I thank you for pointing out to me this serious fault. I ask you to forget the other letter, and to forgive me in God's name.

I am not going to begin again to write on the subject of solitude. It is finished. I have nothing to say. I will try to be a good monk and to live as a solitary the best I can, according to the will of my Superiors. I have always tried to do what my Superiors wanted. I thought I accepted their will last year. And I accept it now. I am not saying this to please you; I am saying this before God, because it is the truth, and I know that you like the truth. I have never tried to flatter my Superiors; I speak to them straightforwardly, as I think. And I accept what is answered to me. Perhaps it is somewhat in the American way that I do that: then, pardon me. You are also a Father; you will understand.

I am going to pay attention to this error you point out to me; I am going to study with care all the aspects of the question. I am going to do all that is possible to correct myself. I beg you to help me with your prayers. I am going to write fewer articles. I will avoid seeking written dialogues with non-Catholics, except for the particular persons whom I can help, in private, to find the faith.

P.S. As I reread the censor's remarks and your good letter, I must tell you all the same that the censor interprets my words in a sense that I certainly did not intend, though I am responsible because of lack of care in my expressions. I must tell you, not to excuse myself, but to testify to my faith in the Holy Church, that I did not want at all to say and I have never thought that a Christian should prefer the interior voice to the voice of obedience!!! What is said on page 29 is not "a direct attack against the Superiors." I don't speak of Superiors in the context *at all.* It is the Father Censor who makes them enter it. But above all on page 28 he has completely *overturned the meaning* of what I meant. I precisely said that the solitary was tormented by agonizing isolation in which he could not have *the security of obedience* to a Superior!!

That is what I said, and meant to say. Of course, since the Father Censor took it in a dangerous sense, I am responsible; I should have been cautious.

I confess that I feel very wounded by this interpretation and by your doubly severe judgment. It is my fault, really, but the wound remains.

In the hands of this Father there are still other manuscripts that he might turn and interpret in this way. I shall change them. I am wrong! But above all do not think that I disobey once again!

Also in the book *The New Man,* written in 1955 and passing only today through the censorship, one will want to change certain expressions one will find somewhat risky maybe. Do not worry! I'll do whatever possible to avoid all that may shock.

(SOC 131–32)

"A Signed Confession of Crimes against the State," 1960

I AM THE KIND OF PERSON who must sooner or later, inevitably, fill pages of blank paper with the confession of secret crimes against the state. Why not be prepared? There is no time like the present—and who, in such a present, can promise himself a future?

My very existence is an admission of guilt. Placed before a blank sheet of paper, any blank sheet of paper, I instinctively begin to set down the list of my latest crimes. What else can I do? The very thoughts of a person like me are crimes against the state. All I have to do is think: and immediately I become guilty. In spite of all my efforts to correct this lamentable tendency to subversiveness and intellectual sabotage, I cannot possibly get rid of it.

What is the good of confessing it again? But that is the least I can do, for, they tell me, everyone must love the state. And those who one way or another have never been able to muster up the slightest interest in the state, must now be made to show either love or hatred. One way or the other. If you don't love, hate. And if you hate, then you can turn your hatred into love by confessing it, and expiating it. If you are fool enough to love, why not go the whole way and immolate yourself with self-accusations? After all, no love of yours can ever be good enough for the state! Unfortunately, my love is lukewarm at best.

Here is a blank sheet of paper. No one is forcing me to do this. I am trying to do it out of "love" (meaning of course hatred). I am trying to convince myself that I am sufficiently interested in the state to hate it.

It is not easy, yet. For this reason I am sometimes tempted to leave the paper the way it is and not write on it at all. Or simply to sign it, and let them write on it later. But no. Red-blooded patriotism will have none of this. Let me confess my secret and subversive desire not to accuse myself. I have but one life and one reputation to lay down for the Nation, the People, and the Party. So let's go.

I declare that everything that I am now about to write will be either true or false, and I confess that neither I nor the state care which, so long as something is written. Everything that is written, anywhere, or by anybody, is a potential confession of crime against the state. Including the official documents of the state itself, the official histories, etc., etc. Everything written down, whether defiant or servile, whether partisan or indifferent, turns in the end into a death warrant. I will mix defiance and servility in the desired proportions and my indifference will make me the partisan of all oppositions.

I confess that I am sitting under a pine tree doing absolutely nothing. I have done nothing for one hour and firmly intend to continue to do nothing for an indefinite period. I have taken my shoes off. I confess that I have been listening to a mockingbird. Yes, I admit that it is a mockingbird. I hear him singing in those cedars, and I am very sorry. It is probably my fault. He is singing again. This kind of thing goes on all the time. Wherever I am, I find myself the center of reactionary plots like this one.

I confess furthermore that there is a tanager around here somewhere.

I do not deny that I have been looking for the tanager and after five minutes I have seen him. I am the only person who has seen this particular tanager at this particular time, since there is nobody else around. I confess that there is nobody else around because I came here on purpose to get away from the state. I avow, in a frantic paroxysm of grief, that the state and I are much better off when we have nothing to do with each other. And I even confess that I (in contradistinction to the state) believe that this separation is not only desirable but even possible. Indeed it is, at least temporarily, an accomplished fact. I confess it. I confess it. The birds are singing again, and I confess it.

(You say that this is indeed horrible, but that it is not yet horrible enough. I am sorry, I cannot improve on the truth. That is a refinement I must leave to the state, which is perfectly equipped to do a very good job of it. I am just writing down what I have actually done, or rather what I have not done. That is usually it: I just *don't do* the things that they do on one side or the other. I am therefore probably worse than all the rest, since I am neither a partisan nor a traitor. The worst traitor is the one who simply takes no interest. That's me. Here I sit in the grass. I watch the clouds go by, and like it. Quisling. Trotsky. Judas.)

I admit that nothing has happened all afternoon, and that it continues to happen. It is true, I have got my feet in an anthill, by mistake. (Ah, now we are getting somewhere!!) I might as well confess it. There are ants on the paper as I write. They are determined to take over all the writing, but meanwhile the sun shines and I am here under the pine trees. While there is still time I confess that there are ants on the paper, and a fly in my ear. I do not try to deny that there is a fly in my ear and another on my sleeve. Honestly I don't care. I am sorry. I have no desire to get rid of them. If I had a grain of true patriotism those flies would make a difference. I beg the forgiveness of the state.

The sun? Yes, it is shining. I see it shine. I am in full agreement with the sunshine. I confess that I have been in sympathy all along with the sun shining, and have not paused for two seconds to consider that it shines on account of the state. I am shattered by the realization that I have never attributed the sunshine to its true cause, namely the state. Clearly I am not worthy to exist another minute. And yet take over all the sunshine, but while there is still time I confess it: the sun is shining.

Signed:

(*Deposition of reliable witness:* He has come to the wood with his shoes in his hand, and with a book. He has sat with papers and a book. He has done no work, but stood and sat in the sun over and around an anthill, at the sound of a bird. The ants are on his hands and feet while he is lying down, standing up, walking about, running, and even running very fast. Yes, there are ants all over the sunshine, running very fast.)

(BOT 65–71)

From a Letter to James Laughlin, August 18, 1961

Laughlin was the founder and editor of New Directions Publishing.

PERSONALLY I AM MORE AND MORE concerned about the question of peace and war. I am appalled by the way everyone simply sits around and acts as though everything were normal. It seems to me that I have an enormous responsibility myself, since I am read by a lot of people, and yet I don't know what to begin to say and then I am as though bound and gagged by the censors, who though not maliciously reactionary are just obtuse and slow. This feeling of frustration is terrible. Yet what can one say? If I go around shouting "abolish war" it will be meaningless. Yet at least someone has to say that. I am in no position to plan a book about it. There is no purpose to a silly book of editorial-like platitudes. Some more poems like Auschwitz, maybe. But the thing is to be *heard*. And everything is perfectly soundproof and thought proof. We are all doped right up to the eyes. And words have become useless, no matter how true they may be. But when it comes to action, then I am more helpless than anyone: except within my own very limited sphere of prayer, with which I have no quarrel at all. That is perhaps the last great power that can do anything: and the less said about it the better. Not only prayer but holiness, which I don't have. We are all wound up in lies and illusions and as soon as we begin to think or talk, the machinery of falsity operates automatically. The worst of all is not to know this, and apparently a lot of people don't.

(TMJL 177)

From a Letter to Dorothy Day, August 23, 1961

Received into the Roman Catholic Church in 1927, Dorothy Day (1897–1980) brought radical social and political convictions with her into the church. Along with Peter Maurin, she founded the Catholic Worker Movement.

I STILL DON'T KNOW what the censors think of the Auschwitz poem ["Chant to Be Used in Processions around a Site with Furnaces"], but there are very good chances that their judgment will be entirely negative: not because of "faith and morals" but because a "Trappist should not know about these things, or should not write about them, etc."

This, Dorothy, is sometimes a very great problem to me. Because I feel obligated to take very seriously what is going on, and to say whatever my conscience seems to dictate, provided of course it is not contrary to the faith and to the teaching authority of the Church. Obedience is a most essential thing in any Christian and above all in a monk, but I sometimes wonder if, being in a situation where obedience would completely silence a person on some important moral issue on which others are also keeping silence—a crucial issue like nuclear war—then I would be inclined to wonder if it were not God's will to ask to change my situation.

Of course, I do not plan this and I know it would be impossible (because I have already tried). I also know that somehow God always makes it possible for me to say what seems to be necessary, and hence there is no question that I am completely in His hands where I am and that I should therefore continue as I am doing. But why this awful silence and apathy on the part of Catholics, clergy, hierarchy, laypeople on this terrible issue on which the very continued existence of the human race depends? As for writing: I don't feel that I can in conscience, at a time like this, go on writing just about things like meditation, though that has its point. I cannot just bury my head in a lot of rather tiny and secondary monastic studies either. I think I have to face the big issues, the life-and-death issues: and this is what everyone is afraid of.

(HGL 139–40)

From a Letter to Father Ronald Roloff, OSB, September 26, 1962

I THINK MOST BENEDICTINES judge my statements almost exclusively in the light of earlier books in which I was much more rigid and doctrinaire than I believe I have since become. There has, I think, been a slight evolution in my thought about the monastic life from *The Waters of Siloe* (which I regard now as a rough and immature essay) to *The Silent Life* and even more recent essays, such as some of those in *Disputed Questions*. What that evolution may have been exactly, I do not attempt to say myself at this point. But I do feel it is a reality, and though I have by my early and more impetuous efforts deserved to get shoved into a pigeonhole, I still meekly protest.

(SOC 146)

From a Letter to Sister Therese Lentfoehr, SDS, February 5, 1961

F RANK DELL'ISOLA came out with an article ["Thomas Merton: Outlines of Growth"] saying my best work was No Man Is an Island and that I haven't done anything good since then: which shows his perspective is all off. Not that I claim to be doing specially good work, but to pick *No Man Is an Island* which is vague and not characteristic, and overlook something like the "Notes on Solitude" in *Disputed Questions* which is what I really have to say . . .

(RTJ 238)

From a Letter to Czeslaw Milosz, March 28, 1961

Y OU ARE ALL TOO RIGHT about the sickness of this society. It is terrible and seems to get worse. I feel nothing but helplessness in my situation: I should, ideally speaking, have a wonderful perspective from which to see things in a different—a Heraclitean—light. But at the same time there is so much confusion around me and in my own self. In monasticism there is a fatal mixture of inspiration and inertia that produces an awful inarticulate guilt in anyone who does not simply bury his head in the sand. You never know when you are right and how far you can go in studying the world outside and reacting to it. There are infinite temptations, the first of which is to think that one is separate from it all and somehow "pure," while really we are full of the same poisons. Hence we fight in ourselves many of the same ambiguities. There is always the temptation to justify ourselves by condemning "the world." You are perfectly right about the "spellbound dance of paralytics." You are right too that they anesthetize themselves with the double-talk of lotus-eaters, the psychological talk: all this talk about responsibility and personalism and organization men and whatnot tends to be a part of the spell and of the dance. What is behind it? The obsession with concepts, with knowledge, with techniques, as if we were supposed to be able to manipulate everything. We have got ourselves into a complete fog of concepts and "answers." Illusory answers to illusory problems and never facing the real problem: that we have all become zombies.

This works on several levels, of course. It is quite obvious on the level of the race fanatics, but on the intellectual level it persists too. I think the Marxist psychology of bourgeois individualism is not too far wrong when it contemns the perpetual turning around and around in circles of guilt and self-analysis: as if this were capable of doing something, or exorcizing the real guilt. . . . But they are in the same boat themselves, only a few stages farther back. They haven't yet got to the stage of idleness and surfeiting that will permit them to do the same thing. The poison is exactly the alienation you speak of and it is not the individual not society but what comes of being an individual helpless to liberate himself from the images that society fills him with. It is a very fine picture of hell sometimes. When I see advertisements I want to curse they make me so sick and I do curse them. I have never seen TV, that is never watched it. Once when I did happen to pass in front of a set, I saw the commercial that was on: two little figures were dancing around worshipping a roll of toilet paper, chanting a hymn in its honor. I think this is symbolic enough, 'isn't it? We have simply lost the ability to see what is right in front of us: things like this need no comment. What I said above does not apply to your revisionists. I don't know much about them, I know Erich Fromm is studying along those lines. Maybe there is some hope there. If there is hope anywhere, it lies somewhere in the middle between the two extremes (which in reality meet). The extremes are closer together than the "middle" which seems to be between them.

When you say I am the only one who can start something in this country, I don't know what to say. It might ideally be true. I should certainly be in such a position. It should be not too difficult to give a brief, searching glance at something like TV and then really say what one has seen. In a way I would like to. Yet I realize that the position is not so simple. For one thing, I am caught by as many nets as anybody else. It is to the interests of the Order to preserve just one kind of definite image of me, and nothing else. Lately I have been expanding on all sides beyond the limits of this approved image. . . . It is not well accepted. Not that I care, but you see there would right away be very effective opposition even to so simple a matter as a study of TV and its evils. "Monks don't watch TV." And so on. For me, however, to raise this one question would mean raising an unlimited series of other questions which I am not yet prepared to face. What I would say is that if you are right, which you may be to some extent, the time is not yet ripe and I have a lot of preparing to do. I can't explain this, but I need to grow more, ripen more. My past work is nowhere near up to the level that would be required to begin something like this. My latest work is not there yet either.

Meanwhile I am going to take a vacation from writing

and do a lot of reading and thinking if I can. It is really vital that I get more into the center of the real problems. I mean the real ones.

What I hope most of all is that you will be able to stop by here and that we will be able to talk. Don't worry about accommodations for your wife and children, they can be put up with friends of mine in Louisville. I do very much want to talk to you and I think it is important that we have a chance to iron out these things as it cannot be done in writing.

You are right that you would never adapt to this country. If you are out of Poland, well, you are out of it. No one knows what the future will bring. Incidentally, I don't know if I have the true picture of what is going on there but it seems to me that the flat intransigence of the Cardinal Primate is in its own way admirable. I am not an integrist and do not want to be one, but I think the Church is right not to fool around with compromises that have no other purpose than her destruction. This at least is an honest reaction: but would that the Church reacted against the other compromises in other countries that pretend to preserve her in a way that leads only to death and to spiritual extinction, infidelity to God.

Speaking in monastic terms, of fidelity to the truth, to the light that is in us from God, that is the horror: everyone has been more or less unfaithful, and those who have seemed to be faithful have been so partially, in a way that sanctified greater evasions (the Grand Inquisitor). Perhaps the great reality of our time is this, that no one is capable of this fidelity, and all have failed in it, and that there is no hope to be looked for in any one of us. But God is faithful. It is what the Holy Week liturgy tells of His "treading the winepress by Himself." This, I think, is the central reality.

(CFT 71–73)

From a Letter to Dorothy Day, July 23, 1961

I BECOME MORE AND MORE SKEPTICAL about my writing. There has been some good and much bad, and I haven't been nearly honest enough and clear enough. The problem that torments me is that I can so easily become part of a general system of delusion. From the moment we are labeled as Catholics and the "Catholic position" also has a label, even our sincere rejection of falsity can be used in the service of falsity, since our label is associated with the system that wants and intends to defend itself—and the glory of God—with bombs. But all the systems are in the same boat, it seems. I find myself more and more drifting toward the derided and probably quite absurd and defeatist position of a sort of Christian anarchist. This of course would be foolish, if I followed it to the end. But it is no less foolish to hang in midair halfway to it. But perhaps the most foolish of all would be to renounce all consideration of any alternative to the status quo, the giant machine. These words on the Sunday of Christ's tears over Jerusalem.

(HGL 139)

From a Letter to Ernesto Cardenal, February 25, 1963

THOUGH I HAVE BEEN QUITE BUSY, I see more and more that the dimension of my life that has meaning is the solitary one, which cannot be expressed. There are things which can and must be communicated, but it is an error to attach too much importance to them. I think it is really a waste of time for me to write more books on "the spiritual life" in the usual sense of the word. I have done enough already. And at the same time it seems futile to write about the way the world is going: yet it is true there are times when one must speak. But one must be sure of the necessity. James Baldwin has written several terrific books about the race situation in this country.

(CFT 139)

From a Letter to Abbot Anthony Chassagne, OCSO, August 21, 1963

Anthony Chassagne entered Gethsemani in 1941 and was a contemporary of Merton's during the years of his noviatiate and studies for the priesthood. He later became superior of the foundation at Mepkin, South Carolina, and elected abbot.

Your Bro. Bonaventure seized me violently in the Prior's room and recited to me some very bad poetry which, in the heat of the moment, I managed to recognize as being by me. In such ways does the good Lord enlighten sinners and sweetly seek to draw them out of darkness.

(SOC 181)

From a letter to Father Kilian McDonnell, December 20, 1963

Kilian McDonnell is a monk of St. John's Abbey, Collegeville, Minnesota.

I am writing mostly monastic essays these days, and studying things like Aetheria's pilgrimage, letters of Anselm, and stuff by Peter the Venerable and Peter of Celles, along with Desert Fathers here and there. With poetry on the side, and I would like to continue to translate some South American poets, if I get time. My "ecumenical" bent seems to be more toward the people who have *nothing,* the poets and intellectuals and the Zen set. This I think is more my line, and yet perhaps this does not rate as "ecumenism." I don't intend however to get discussing too much with them either. What I can do for them can be done by writing, I think.

(SOC 190)

From a letter to "My Dear Friend," ca. 1963

The following is a form letter sent out to those, especially students, who wrote requesting basic facts about Merton's life and writings.

A T ONE TIME I THOUGHT I ought to give up writing poetry because it might not be compatible with the life of a monk, but I don't think this anymore. People ask me how I write poetry. I just write it. I get an idea and I put it down, and add to it, and take away what is useless, and try to end up with some kind of poem. A poem is for me the expression of an inner poetic experience, and what matters is the experience, more than the poem itself. Some of my favorite poets are St.-John Perse [Alexis Léger], F. García Lorca, Dylan Thomas, Gerard Manley Hopkins, Boris Pasternak, William Blake, John Donne, Dante, Shakespeare, Tu Fu, Isaias, Aeschylus, Sophocles, etc.

(RTJ 90)

From a Letter to Dom Jean-Baptiste Porion, March 26, 1964

A S I REFLECT OVER the past and over God's grace in my life there are only two things that are more or less certain to me: that I have been called to be at once a writer and

a solitary *secundum quid* [in some way]. The rest is confusion and uncertainty. At present however I do have a measure of solitude, more than I would have expected in the
past, and it is the only thing that helps me to keep sane. I
am grateful for this gift from God, with all the paradoxes
that it entails and its peculiar interior difficulties, as well as
its hidden and dry joys. I think that really there is no solitude but a solitude *secundum quid,* lodged in paradox, and
that one becomes a solitary in proportion as he can accept
the paradox and the irony of his position. It is the irony that
is the expression of God's love in the life of the "monazon"
[one who lives alone], the one who practices loneliness on
purpose. The joy of the solitary is then the laughter that
makes him, as the Fathers said, an Isaac, *thus,* a joke and a
delight of the humor of the Lord. I wish you this joy at
Easter, and know that I owe my share of it in part to your
prayers.

(SOC 211)

From a Letter to Dame Marcella Van Bruyn, June 16, 1965

*Dame Marcella Van Bruyn was a hermitess; she entered
Stanbrook Abbey in England when she was forty-five,
and after twenty-three years of monastic life, she left to
lead a solitary life.*

I HOPE GRADUALLY to give up writing. I don't plan to cut
it off all of a sudden, because I know myself well
enough to realize that this activity is helpful to me and in
no way interferes with a genuine life of prayer. It has always been a help, the writing part. The publication problems are a little more distracting. But I think eventually

the writing will die out by itself. I can see now that I would soon begin to lose interest. But I will probably always write a few little things like meditations or poems, on the spur of the moment.

As to correspondence, that too will gradually work itself out, I hope. At the moment I have a great load of it, with all kinds of letters from strangers, people wanting direction and so on. Most of it I cannot answer, and I do not try. Next year I would want to cut it down to just proportions. It seems to me, though that "just proportions" includes keeping up a monastic correspondence, within reason. Obviously not a continued barrage, but occasional necessary letters on points of some interest. Your question would be a case in point.

(SOC 284)

From a Letter to Antoinette M. Costa, May 13, 1965

Antoinette Costa was a high school student from Taunton, Massachusetts, writing a school paper on Merton's poetry.

ABOUT THOSE EARLY CRITICS: it is difficult for me to have any kind of opinion, as no one can judge rightly in his own case. The best thing I can do is say, as objectively as I can, that I felt they were writing about somebody who wasn't there. They had not heard me, they had heard somebody else, and they had not read what I had intended to write. This of course often happens. The whole question of communication is a very difficult one, and most difficult when one writes imaginatively and symbolically as I do. There is a whole class of people who simply react negatively to my kind of thought and my kind of writing. This is not surprising, and it is as it should be. I for my part have absolutely no interest in them either, they seem to me to be prosaic and stupid, and to have very little feeling for what seems to me to be real. They tend to be rationalists, materialists, or else stolid traditionalists of an external type. To these I have nothing to say.

As for [Frank] Dell'Isola's statement [in "The Conversion and Growth of Thomas Merton"] that *No Man Is an Island* changed the minds of critics, I don't know. I do know however that one of my early critics, Dom Aelred Graham, did change his mind around that point and what happened was that we both came to see that we really agreed. He is English and I write in tones that some English people get offended at, because it seems to them to be too aggressive ("strident") but since Dom Aelred wrote *Zen Catholicism,* which I liked very much, and which I praised [in "Zen: Sense and Sensibility"], we are on very good terms and see that we agree.

Yes, I am writing articles and poems now, and I have a new book on the race question and peace which has also been criticized, *Seeds of Destruction.* I have an article ["Rain and the Rhinoceros"] in the May issue of *Holiday* if you are interested in what is new down this way. God bless you and good luck with your paper.

(RTJ 335)

From *"Answers on Art and Freedom,"* 1965

I DO NOT CONSIDER MYSELF integrated in the war-making society of which I live, but the problem is that this society *does* consider *me* integrated in it. I notice that for nearly twenty years my society—or those in it who read my books—have decided upon an identity for me and insist that I continue to correspond perfectly to the idea of me which they found upon reading my first successful book. Yet the same people simultaneously prescribe for me a contrary identity. They demand that I remain forever the superficially pious, rather rigid, and somewhat narrow-minded young monk I was twenty years ago, and at the same time they continually circulate the rumor that I have left my monastery. What has actually happened is that I have been simply living where I am and developing in my own way without consulting the public about it, since it is none of the public's business.

(LE 378–79)

From Conjectures of a Guilty Bystander, *1966*

F OR MY OWN PART I consider myself neither conservative nor an extreme progressive. I would like to think I am what Pope John was—a progressive with a deep respect and love for tradition—In other words a progressive who wants to preserve a very clear and marked *continuity* with the past and not make silly and idealistic compromises with the present—yet to be *completely open* to the modern world while retaining the clearly defined, traditionally Catholic position.

(CGB 312)

From a Letter to Dom Jean Leclercq, November 18, 1966

R EFLECTION ON MY CRITICS once again: Of course they have no trouble at all finding faults in me since I have frankly discussed my own faults in public. An *ad personam* [an attack on *the person* not the argument] argument is not too difficult under such circumstances. I would however like to see them meet me on my own ground. Let them write spiritual journals as frank as mine and see if they will meet the test of publication.

(SOC 321–22)

From a Letter to Mother Angela Collins, December 1, 1966

I WON'T GIVE UP WRITING. I can't; I have too many odd jobs I have to do all the time. But I just have no desire whatever to get down to another book, though I finished a crazy book of poems recently. That's different. And I don't really want to write much about "spiritual things" either. That least of all, in fact. I have gradually developed a sort of nausea for talking about it. Except when I really have to. The words sound too empty and trivial. Not that I am immersed in something marvelous: I just live and don't feel like spinning out a lot of words about life or God or prayer. I feel in fact immensely poor and fallible but don't worry about it. Just live. Still, I suppose a lot of stuff does get turned out: do you receive the mimeographed material that they send out? I might as well send you a copy of the new book—*Conjectures*—hoping you don't have it already. I will send it along with this. A Christmas present.

(SOC 323)

From a Circular Letter: Septuagesima Sunday 1967

MORE AND MORE since living alone I have wanted to stop fighting, and arguing, and proclaiming and criticizing. I think the points on which protest has been demanded of me and given by me are now well enough known. Obviously there may be other such situations in the future. In a world like ours—a world of war, riot, murder, racism, tyranny, and established banditry, one has to be able to stand up and say NO. But there are also other things to do. I am more and more convinced of the reality of my own job which is meditation and study and prayer in silence. I do not intend to give up writing, that too is obviously my vocation. But I hope I will be able to give up controversy some day. Pray for me. When one gets older (Jan. 31 is my fifty-second birthday) one realizes the futility of a life wasted in argument when it should be given entirely to love.

(RTJ 97)

From a Circular Letter: Midsummer 1967

MORE AND MORE the cards I have been putting on the table have been saying: "I don't know the answers, but I have some questions I'd like to share with you." There is always an implication that it means something to know the questions, especially if they are common questions. But now I am beginning to wonder if I even know the questions, or if they are common to others. In such a case one eventually gets around to saying: "Since I don't know where it all begins, I'd better just shut up." Of course, it will not be that easy to shut me up: I am writing less, but still writing. No doubt the writing will tend to get further out and less popular. And I still recognize some obligation to take up a position on this or that moral issue of general urgency, not because I claim to have the answer, but because one has to take a responsible stand. Stupidity and evasion are no excuse from complicity in what goes on in the world of today. To have lived under Hitler and merely ignored the death camps is not an enviable moral position.

(RTJ 104–5)

From a Circular Letter: Easter 1967

B ESIDES MY ORDINARY WORK I now have on my desk the following: One complete manuscript of a novel on which I am asked to comment by a publisher. A set of galleys of a book on Zen, ditto. Several chapters of a book on mysticism to read and criticize. A long statement on the Vietnam War I am supposed to sign (generally I don't sign any of these statements, because I can't read the papers or watch TV to keep up as others do). A list of twenty-four magazine articles which I must either read and report on myself, or get others to summarize, for the magazine of the Order. A book review article of six or seven books on Camus, in state of outline, to be written somehow in the next week or so. At least two books to review for the magazine of the Order. (I mention only the two that happen to be directly visible at the moment. There are probably others on the shelf behind me or buried under the mass of other material that confronts me.) Finally, on top of that, I have an urgent report to write on an official matter, and am requested to give this top priority. And so on. The life of a writing hermit is certainly not one of lying around in the sun or of pious navel gazing. Nevertheless there is the question of meditation which, to me, is always the first thing of all because without it the rest becomes meaningless. In such circumstances, writing letters, receiving visits, and so on would simply complicate matters beyond all reasonable measure.

(RTJ 100)

From a Letter to Sister J. M.,
June 17, 1968

She wrote to Merton asking him about the stages of his writing.

DURING THE FIRST PERIOD, after entering the monastery, I was totally isolated from all outside influences and was largely working with what I had accumulated before entering. [I drew] on the experience of the monastic life in my early days when I was quite ascetic, "first fervor" stuff, and when the life at Gethsemani was very strict. This resulted in a highly unworldly, ascetical, intransigent, somewhat apocalyptic outlook. Rigid, arbitrary separation between God and the world, etc. Most people judge me entirely by this period, either favorably or unfavorably, and do not realize that I have changed a great deal. The second period was a time when I began to open up again to the world, began reading psychoanalysis (Fromm, Horney, etc.), Zen Buddhism, existentialism, and other things like that, also more literature.

. . . Yes, I have a lot of critics, particularly among Catholics. These are usually people who have seen one aspect of my work which they don't like. Most of them are put off by the fact that I sound at times like a Catholic Norman Mailer. I get on better with non-Catholics, particularly the younger generation, students, hippies, etc. At the same time there is always a solid phalanx of people who seem to get a lot out of the early books up to about *Thoughts in Solitude,* and have never heard of the others. These tend to be people interested in the spiritual life and somewhat conservative in many ways. Hence the curious fact that there are by and large two Mertons: one ascetic, conservative, traditional, monastic. The other radical, independent, and somewhat akin to beats and hippies and to poets in general. Neither one of these appeals to the current pace-setters for Catholic thought and life in the U.S. today. Some of them respect me, others think I'm nuts, none of them really dig me. Which is perfectly all right. Where I fit seems to be in the sort of niche provided by the *Catholic Worker*—and outside that, well, the literary magazines whether little or otherwise. Mostly little. And New Directions [the publishing house], where I have always been.

I guess that's about it. Looking back on my work, I wish I had never bothered to write about one-third of it—the books that tend to be (one way or the other) "popular" religion. Or "inspirational." But I'll stand by things like *Seeds of Contemplation* (as emended in *New Seeds*). *Seven Storey Mountain* is a sort of phenomenon, not all bad, not all good, and it's not something I could successfully repudiate even if I wanted to. Naturally I have reservations about it because I was young then and I've changed.

(SOC 384–85)

From a Circular Letter: Midsummer 1968

SEVERAL MAGAZINES asked me to write something concerning the assassination of Robert Kennedy. I refused because I am a bit suspicious of what seems to me to be a growing ritual cycle: murder, public acts of contrition, deploring violence, gestures of appeasement, then everything goes on unchanged and presently there is another assassination. The cycle continues. The sickness seems to be so deep that ritual expressions of sorrow, horror, astonishment, etc., have just become part of a general routine. At such a time perhaps silence is more decent.

(RTJ, 115–16)

Advice to Writers

From The Inner Experience, *1959*

THE WORST THING that can happen to a man who is already divided up into a dozen different compartments is to seal off yet another compartment and tell him that this one is more important than all the others, and that he must henceforth exercise a special care in keeping it separate from them. . . .

The first thing that you have to do, before you even start thinking about such a thing as contemplation, is to try to recover your basic natural unity, to *reintegrate* your compartmentalized being into a coordinated and simple whole and learn to live as a unified *human person*. This means that you have to bring back together the fragments of your distracted existence so that when you say "I," there is really someone present to support the pronoun you have uttered. Reflect, sometimes, on the disquieting fact that most of your statements of opinions, tastes, deeds, desires, hopes, and fears are statements about someone who is not really present. When you say "I think," it is often not you who think, but "they"—it is the anonymous authority of the collectivity speaking through your mask. When you say "I want," you are sometimes simply making an automatic gesture of accepting, paying for, what has been forced upon you. That is to say, you reach out for what you have been made to want.

(IE 2, 3–4)

From New Seeds of Contemplation, *1961*

I F YOU WRITE FOR GOD you will reach many men and bring them joy.

If you write for men—you may make some money and you may give someone a little joy and you may make a noise in the world, for a little while.

If you write only for yourself, you can read what you yourself have written and after ten minutes you will be so disgusted you will wish that you were dead.

(NS 111)

• • •

If a writer is so cautious that he never writes anything that cannot be criticized, he will never write anything that can be read. If you want to help other people you have got to make up your mind to write things that some men will condemn.

(NS 105)

From a Letter to Jacques Maritain,
June 11, 1963

D O NOT PUSH TOO HARD with the work, God will take care of everything, and will give you strength to do all that needs to be done. The rest is in His hands. Realize yourself to be entirely in His love and His care and worry about nothing. In these days you should be carried by Him toward your destination, and do what you do more as play than as work, which does not mean that it is not serious: for the most serious thing in the life of a Christian is play. The seriousness of Christian play is the only genuine seriousness. Our work, when it develops the seriousness of worldly accomplishment, is sad indeed, and it does nothing. But of course it is normal to work "against the clock" when one's time is clearly measured, and to feel anxiety about not finishing. But this too is part of God's play in our life, and we will see it in the end. It is like the book of Tobias, that beautiful book about God's play in the life of man, and in the troubles of man. All life is in reality the playing and dancing of the Child-God in His world, and we, alas, have not seen it and known it.

That is the real tragedy of the cold war and the nuclear weapons: the tragic false seriousness of the devil and his frenzy, his Babel-building, his technology, his vulcanism. True, we must find spirituality even in this kind of context, but it is such a pitiful confusion, so full of temptations (Teilhard [de Chardin] made an attempt, and it is pitifully naïve in its confusions and its goodwill). But the real sorrow is this awful jigging of machines, and this construction of colossi. Do you ever see the *Scientific American*? It is really an excellent magazine, and the articles are well done, but the *advertising* is phenomenal! What naked hubris! Advertising is one of the great *loci classici* [classic categories] for the theology of the devil. There his hand is quite clear, with all his tropes and myths and figures and signs and all his own personal Midrash.

(CFT 38)

From a Letter to Lorraine,
April 17, 1964

Y OU ASK HOW a Catholic writer can have "the greatest possible influence on his public." A seemingly innocent question, but to a writer, and to one in my position, it is more complex than it appears.

What do you mean "his public"? The writer's "public" is a very mysterious entity and it is certainly different from the Publisher's Public and the Reviewer's Public. There is a public that reads the blurb on the jacket and then, if it reads the book at all, sees it only in the light of the blurb—or the review which copied the blurb. If that is the public one is to "influence" then what matters is to have good blurbs and lots of advertising and bang-up reviews, and if possible a pretty good and original image of the writer himself.

This, of course, is a waste of time and an indignity, and is not worthy of consideration in a serious man's mind.

The writer who has "influence" on the people who really need to read him must have something important to say, and something that is important *now* or perhaps tomorrow, later than now. And he must want to say it to the men of his time, perhaps even to others later. But it must be a bit desperate if it is going to get out at all. And if it is desperate, it will be opposed. Hence no writer who has anything important to say can avoid being opposed and criticized. Thus the writer who wants to—let us say reach, or help rather than influence people—must suffer for the truth of his witness and for love of the people he is reaching. Otherwise his communion with them is shallow and without life. The real writer lives in deep communion with his readers, because they share in common sufferings and desires and needs that are *urgent*.

Of course the writer has to be articulate and he has to write well. He has to take his craft seriously. As for the Catholic writer, he has got to do something better than to put the catechism in a new form that will appear to be "catchy." He may have to say some things that shock his fellow Catholics. I don't claim that he says *nothing but* these things that shock, but sometimes he may have to.

(WTF 167)

From "Message to Poets," February 1964

W E MUST REFUSE academic classification. We must reject the seductions of publicity. We must not allow ourselves to be pitted one against another in mystical comparisons—political, literary, or cultural orthodoxies. We must not be made to devour and dismember one another for the amusement of their press. We must not let ourselves be eaten by them to assuage their own insatiable doubt. We must not merely be *for* something and *against* something else, even if we are for "ourselves" and against them. Who are they? Let us not give them support by becoming an "opposition" which assumes they are definitively real.

Let us remain outside "their" categories. It is in this sense that we are all monks: for we remain innocent and invisible to publicists and bureaucrats. They cannot imagine what we are doing unless we betray ourselves to them, and even then they will never be able.

They understand nothing except what they themselves have decreed. They are crafty ones who weave words about life and then make life conform to what they themselves have declared. How can they trust anyone when they make life itself tell lies? It is the businessman, the propagandist, the politician, not the poet, who devoutly believes in "the magic of words."

(LE 372–73)

From a Letter to John O'Keefe, November 4, 1965

O'Keefe wrote to Merton from Dublin, Ireland, asking what advice he would give to a young aspiring writer.

THIS WILL BE BRIEF INDEED, but in charity I will at least try to send you something. In writing for ordinary people (what other people are there?) I would say do this:

1. Never write down to anyone.

2. Never write simply what you think they want.

3. Write rather what is deepest in your own heart and what you know—as a writer has an instinct by which to know this—is also deep in theirs. In other words, write to elucidate problems that are common and urgent.

4. Write only after you have thoroughly learned what you want to say—but this has to be qualified. By all means practice. Why not write a novel? Except maybe you have not time. Try a story or two. But don't just write like "a Short Story Writer," or a pro of some sort.

5. Ireland has great writers, very articulate writers. Read them: I am sure you do. I do not now mean some of my former scandalous favorites like Joyce, but so many others from Yeats and Synge to Brendan Behan (don't be scandalized).

And now you can do me a favor: what is the best bookstore in Dublin for getting source material on Irish monasticism, things perhaps out of print, like the *Rule of*

Tallaght, which I need badly? I would be grateful for such information.

(RTJ 335–36)

From The Way of Chuang Tzu, *1965*

THE MORE ONE SEEKS "the good" outside oneself as something to be acquired, the more one is faced with the necessity of discussing, studying, understanding, analyzing the nature of the good. The more, therefore, one becomes involved in abstractions and in the confusion of divergent opinions. The more "the good" is objectively analyzed, the more it is treated as something to be attained by special virtuous techniques, the less real it becomes. As it becomes less real, it recedes further into the distance of abstraction, futurity, unattainability. The more, therefore, one concentrates on the means to be used to attain it. And as the end becomes more remote and more difficult, the means become more elaborate and complex, until finally the mere study of the means becomes so demanding that all one's effort must be concentrated on this, and the end is forgotten. Hence the nobility of the Ju[7] scholar becomes, in reality, a devotion to the systematic uselessness of practicing means which lead nowhere. This is, in fact, nothing but organized despair: "the good" that is preached and exacted by the moralist thus finally becomes an evil, and all the more so since the hopeless pursuit of it distracts one from the real good which one already possesses and which one now despises or ignores.

(WOC 23)

---

7. Merton is referring here to heroic and self-sacrificing public servants formed in the school of Confucius.—Ed.

• • •

In the age when life on earth was full, no one paid any special attention to worthy men, nor did they single out the man of ability. Rulers were simply the highest branches on the tree, and the people were like deer in the woods. They were honest and righteous without realizing that they were "doing their duty." They loved each other and did not know that this was "love of neighbor." They deceived no one yet they did not know that they were "men to be trusted." They were reliable and did not know that this was "good faith." They lived freely together giving and taking, and did not know that they were generous. For this reason their deeds have not been narrated. They made no history.

(WOC 76)

• • •

THE WOODCARVER

Khing, the master carver, made a bell stand
Of precious wood. When it was finished,
All who saw it were astounded. They said it
    must be
The work of spirits.
The Prince of Lu said to the master carver:
"What is your secret?"

Khing replied: "I am only a workman:
I have no secret. There is only this:
When I began to think about the work you
    commanded
I guarded my spirit, did not expend it
On trifles, that were not to the point.
I fasted in order to set

My heart at rest.
After three days fasting,
I had forgotten gain and success.
After five days
I had forgotten praise or criticism.
After seven days
I had forgotten my body
With all its limbs.

"By this time all thought of your Highness
And of the court had faded away.
All that might distract me from the work
Had vanished.
I was collected in the single thought
Of the bell stand.

"Then I went to the forest
To see the trees in their own natural state.
When the right tree appeared before my eyes,
The bell stand also appeared in it, clearly,
    beyond doubt.
All I had to do was to put forth my hand
And begin.

"If I had not met this particular tree
There would have been
No bell stand at all.

"What happened?
My own collected thought
Encountered the hidden potential in the wood;
From this live encounter came the work
Which you ascribe to the spirits."

(WOC 110–11)

• • •

From "WHEN THE SHOE FITS"

Easy is right. Begin right
And you are easy.
Continue easy and you are right.
The right way to go easy
Is to forget the right way
And forget that the going is easy.

(WOC 113)

• • •

From "THE EMPTY BOAT"

A wise man has said:
"He who is content with himself
Has done a worthless work.
Achievement is the beginning of failure.
Fame is the beginning of disgrace."

Who can free himself from achievement
And from fame, descend and be lost
Amid the masses of men?
He will flow like Tao, unseen,
He will go about like Life itself
With no name and no home.
Simple is he, without distinction.
To all appearances he is a fool.
His steps leave no trace. He has no power.
He achieves nothing, has no reputation.
Since he judges no one
No one judges him.
Such is the perfect man:
His boat is empty.

(WOC 115)

From a Circular Letter:
Christmas 1966

To THE MANY who have written to ask me about their poetry, how to get it published and so on. As if I knew!! Some of the best poets in the country have great difficulty getting their poems published commercially in book form. Most of their stuff appears in little magazines, and a lot of it is circulated in mimeograph or other cheap processes. This is the best thing to do with your poetry, this and reading it in coffeehouses and so on. The idea that anything good has to appear between hard covers is a pure myth and you should stop being obsessed by it. Do you want to be *read* or do you want to have the imagined "status" of a book publication that may or may not mean being read? If you want to be read, get your stuff into the hands of those who are likely to be interested, in any form you can. You yourself have to find out who is likely to be interested in *your* poems. I can't tell you, it is a question of your own relationships, part of your own life.

(RTJ 94)

From a Letter to Ernesto Cardenal,
March 11, 1967

BASICALLY OUR FIRST DUTY today is to human truth in its existential reality, and this sooner or later brings us into confrontation with system and power which seek to overwhelm truth for the sake of particular interests, perhaps rationalized as ideals. Sooner or later this human duty presents itself in a form of crisis that cannot be evaded. At such a time it is very good, almost essential, to have at one's side others with a similar determination, and one can then be guided by a common inspiration and a communion in truth. Here true strength can be found. A completely isolated witness is much more difficult and dangerous. In the end that too may become necessary. But in any case we know that our only ultimate strength is in the Lord and in His Spirit, and faith must make us depend entirely on His will and providence. One must then truly be detached and free in order not to be held and impeded by anything secondary or irrelevant. Which is another way of saying that poverty also is our strength.

(CFT 159)

From "Message of Contemplatives to the World," August 21, 1967

THE MESSAGE OF HOPE the contemplative offers you, then, brother, is not that you need to find your way through the jungle of language and problems that today surround God: but that whether you understand or not, God loves you, is present in you, lives in you, dwells in you, calls you, saves you, and offers you an understanding and light which are like nothing you ever found in books or heard in sermons. The contemplative has nothing to tell you except to reassure you and say that if you dare to penetrate your own silence and risk the sharing of that solitude with the lonely other who seeks God through you, then you will truly recover the light and the capacity to understand what is beyond words and beyond explanations because it is too close to be explained: it is the intimate union in the depths of your own heart, of God's spirit and your own secret inmost self, so that you and He are in all truth One Spirit. I love you, in Christ.

(HGL 158)

From *"Cables to the Ace"*

"THE TRUE WORD of eternity is spoken only in the spirit of that man who is himself a wilderness." (Eckhart)

(CP 453)

ACKNOWLEDGMENTS

GRATEFUL ACKNOWLEDGMENT is made to the following publishers for permission to reprint from copyrighted material:

Excerpts from *No Man Is an Island* by Thomas Merton, copyright 1955 by The Abbey of Our Lady of Gethsemani and renewed 1983 by The Trustees of the Merton Legacy Trust. Reprinted by permission of Harcourt, Inc.

Excerpts from *The Seven Storey Mountain* by Thomas Merton, copyright 1948 by Harcourt, Inc. and renewed 1976 by The Trustees of the Merton Legacy Trust. Reprinted by permission of the publisher.

Excerpts from *Disputed Questions* by Thomas Merton. San Diego: Harcourt, Brace, Jovanovich, 1985. Reprinted by permission of Harcourt, Brace, Jovanovich.

Excerpts from *The Hidden Ground of Love: Letter on Religious Experience and Social Concerns* edited by Willian H. Shannon. San Diego: Harcourt, Brace, Jovanovich, 1985. Reprinted by permission of Harcourt, Brace, Jovanovich.

Excerpts from *The Sign of Jonas* by Thomas Merton,

Trust. Reprinted by permission of New Directions Publishing Corp.

"Cables to the Ace" (excerpt) by Thomas Merton from *The Collected Poems of Thomas Merton,* copyright © 1968 by The Abbey of Gethsemani, Inc. Reprinted by permission of New Directions Publishing Corp.

Various excerpts by Thomas Merton from *The Literary Essays of Thomas Merton,* edited by Patrick Hart, copyright © 1960, 1966, 1967, 1968, 1973, 1975, 1978, 1981 by The Trustees of the Merton Legacy Trust; copyright © 1959, 1961, 1963, 1964, 1965, 1981 by The Abbey of Gethsemani, Inc.; copyright © 1953 by Our Lady of Gethsemani Monastery. Reprinted by permission of New Directions Publishing Corp.

"Sentences" (excerpt) by Thomas Merton from *New Seeds of Contemplation,* copyright © 1961 by The Abbey of Gethsemani, Inc. Reprinted by permission of New Directions Publishing Corp.

"Letter to an Innocent Bystander" (excerpt) by Thomas Merton from *Raids on the Unspeakable,* copyright © 1966 by The Abbey of Gethsemani, Inc. Reprinted by permission of New Directions Publishing Corp.

"The Empty Boat" (excerpt), "The Way of Chuang Tzu: A Study of Chuang Tzu" (excerpt), "The Woodcarver," "When Life Was Full There Was No History," "When the Shoe Fits" (excerpt) by Thomas Merton from *The Way of Chuang Tzu,* copyright © 1965 by The Abbey of Gethsemani. Inc. Reprinted by permission of New Directions Publishing Corp.

Various excerpts by Thomas Merton from *The Wisdom of the Desert,* copyright © 1960 by The Abbey of Gethsemani, Inc. Reprinted by permission of New Directions Publishing Corp.

Excerpts from *A Thomas Merton Reader,* edited by Thomas P. McDonnell, copyright © 1974 by The Trustees of the Merton Legacy Trust. Used by permission of Doubleday, a division of Random House, Inc.

Excerpts from *Conjectures of a Guilty Bystander* by Thomas Merton, copyright ©1966 by The Abbey of Gethsemani, Inc. Used by permission of Doubleday, a division of Random House, Inc.

Excerpts from *My Argument with the Gestapo* by Thomas Merton, copyright © 1969 by The Abbey of Gethsemani, Inc. Used by permission of Doubleday, a division of Random House, Inc.

Excerpts from *Disputed Questions* by Thomas Merton. New York: Harcourt, Brace, Jovanovich, 1960. Excerpts reprinted by permission of the Merton Legacy Trust.

Excerpts from *Honorable Reader*, edited by Robert E. Daggy. New York: Crossroad, 1989. Excerpts reprinted by permission of the Merton Legacy Trust.

Excerpts from *When Prophecy Still Had a Voice* by Thomas Merton, edited by Arthur W. Biddle. Reprinted by permission of the Merton Legacy Trust.

Excerpts from *The Courage for Truth: The Letter of Thomas Merton to Writers* selected and edited by Christine M. Bochen. New York: Farrar, Straus & Giroux, 1993. Reprinted by permission of Farrar, Straus & Giroux.

Excerpts from *The Nonviolent Alternative* (a revised edition of *Thomas Merton on Peace*) edited with an introduction by Gordon C. Zahn. New York: Farrar, Straus & Giroux, 1980. Reprinted by permission of Farrar, Straus & Giroux.

Excerpts from *The Road to Joy: The Letters of Thomas Merton to New and Old Friends* selected and edited by Robert E. Daggy. New York: Farrar, Straus and Giroux & 1989. Reprinted by permission of Farrar, Straus & Giroux.

Excerpts from *Witness to Freedom: The Letters of Thomas Merton in Times of Crisis* selected and edited by William H. Shannon. New York: Farrar, Straus & Giroux, 1994. Reprinted by permission of Farrar, Straus & Giroux.